LIFE IN THE UK TEST
MADE EASY
3RD EDITION

DA ZARATE-ROBB

PUBLISHED BY
Blesilda Zarate-Robb
33 Inveralmond Drive
Edinburgh
United Kingdom
EH4 6JX
twitter account : @myblessbooks

COVER
'A Case History' Sculpture - suitcases cast in concrete with labels of
notable individuals and institutions linked with Liverpool
- Liverpool College of Art
Hope Street, Liverpool.

ISBN
978-0-9563339-1-9

Printed in the United Kingdom

For those who strive to make it in
the United Kingdom
and
for those the United Kingdom
strives for …

Blesilda Zarate-Robb

To God Be the Glory!

TABLE OF CONTENTS

ABOUT THE LIFE IN THE UK TEST

All information in this section is taken from the official website.
For the latest update, visit : www.gov.uk/life-in-the-uk-test/overview

What	The Life in the UK Test, is part of your application for : British citizenship (Naturalisation) or Settlement (Indefinite Leave to Remain).
Why	To show knowledge about Life in the UK.
Who	Applicants for British citizenship (Naturalisation) or Settlement (Indefinite Leave to Remain) in the UK. You do not need to take the test if you are : under eighteen (18) or over sixty-five (65).
When	Must be taken before you apply for Settlement or Naturalisation.
Where	Take the Life in the UK Test only at the accredited / official test centre. There are around sixty (60) test centres. You must choose a test centre close to where you live.
Preparation	Get hold of the official handbook, or Life in the UK Test Made Easy 3rd Edition. Study it right away! Read, absorb, remember.
Test Questions	Questions are based on all parts of the official handbook Life in the United Kingdom A Guide for New Residents 3rd Edition.
Disability	You can make special requests when you book your test. Test centres provide support if you have a disability and need extra equipment to access the centre (do tell your test supervisor).
Cost	£50 (at the time of writing). Latest info can be checked at : www.gov.uk/life-in-the-uk-test/overview
Before booking	Find as much information as you can before booking. Make sure that you have read and understood the information contained at : www.lifeintheuktest.gov.uk

Help with booking	If you need help with your booking, you can contact the : Life in the UK Test Helpline 0800 015 4245 Monday to Friday 8.00 am to 4.00 pm
Booking	Your booking must be at least seven (7) days in advance. You can book the Life in the UK Test online, using the official website only : www.gov.uk/life-in-the-uk-test/overview You must have an email address, debit or credit card and an accepted form of ID. The name you give on your test booking must be an exact match with the name on the ID you use to book the test. You must include any middle names on the booking form or your test will be rejected and you will not get a refund.
IDs when booking	One of the following as ID to book the test : Passport - it can be out of date UK photo card driving licence - full or provisional Convention Travel Document (CTD) Certificate of Identity Document (CID) Stateless Person Document (SPD) EU Identity Card Immigration Status Document endorsed with a UK residence permit on a passport with a photo - it can be out of date Biometric Residence Permit.
Without the above ID	You can email for help if you do not have any of the above documents at : nationalityenquiries@homeoffice.gsi.gov.uk
ID requirements	Acceptable forms of Identification must be Original Documents only. ID documents must contain photos that are a true likeness of you. The ID document presented on the day of the test and used to validate must be the same document used to register and book your Life in the UK Test online. The details displayed on screen must be as stated on the ID you provided and verbally confirmed. That is unless a UK Marriage Certificate, valid UK Spouse Visa in a Passport (within date) or a UK Deed Poll (this must show a red seal) is presented to support this.

Acceptable IDs	Passport from country of origin - this may be out of date.
	United Kingdom and Northern Ireland photo card driving licence (Full or Provisional) - this must be in date.
	Immigration Status Document (ISD), endorsed with a UK Residence Permit (UKRP) bearing a photo of the holder - this may be out of date.
	A UKRP's are only acceptable when affixed to an Immigration Status Document and not within a Passport. Candidates in possession of a Passport containing a UKRP should select the 'Passport option'.
	Convention Travel Document (CTD), which is a blue-cover document similar to a UK passport - this must be in date.
	Stateless Persons Travel Document (SPD), this has a red cover similar to a UK passport - this must be in date.
	Certificate of Identity (CIDs) - this must be in date.
	European Union (EU) Identity Card - this must be in date.
	Biometric Residence Permit Card - this must be in date. BRP's are standalone and not affixed to any other documents.
IDs / documents to bring	You must bring the same ID that you used to book the test. You must also bring proof of address with your name and post code on it.
	From 01 February 2015, documents must be dated within three (3) months of the day of your test - this can be : gas, electricity or water bill Council Tax bill letter from the Home Office with your name and address on it UK photo card driving licence bank or credit card statement (bank statement printed copy must be stamped and signed by the issuing branch).

Incorrect Documents	If you do not bring the correct documents, you will not be able to sit the test and you will not get a refund.
Format	Computer-based.
No. of Questions	You have twenty-four (24) questions.
Types of Questions	Select one (1) correct answer Select two (2) correct answers Select the correct statement Select whether a statement is 'True' or 'False'.
Duration	Forty-five (45) minutes.
To pass the test	You have to answer eighteen (18) questions correctly.
Passing percentage	75% or more to pass the Life in the UK Test.
Result	Either 'Pass' or 'Fail'.
Score	You will not be told of your score.
Passing the test	You only need to pass the test once. If you already passed it as part of your settlement application, you do not need to do it again if you are applying to become a British citizen.
When you pass the test	You will get a 'Pass Notification Letter'.
Pass Notification Letter	You will only get one (1) copy of the letter. You must send the original with your citizenship or settlement application to prove you passed. You will not get a new one if you lose the 'Pass Letter'. Contact the Home Office and they will tell you what to do : Home Office Lost Pass Letters 03001 232 253

Failing the test	You can take the test as many times as you need to. You will need to book and pay again each time.
Taking the test again	You must wait seven (7) days before taking the test again if you fail the test.
Cancellation	You must cancel if you cannot attend the test you booked. You must cancel seven (7) days or more before the date of the test. To cancel the test, you must sign into your Life in the UK account. Click 'My test' from the left-hand menu and click 'Cancel test'. You can ask for a refund if the test centre cancels the test because of flood or no internet connection.
Refund	When cancellation is seven (7) days or more before the date of the test, you can get a refund. The fee will be refunded to the card you originally used to book the test. You can then book a test on another date. You are not eligible for a refund because of : illness, wrong ID, lateness or wrong documents. Download and fill in the refund request form and send it to the address on the form. Refund application must be within three (3) months of the test date.
Complaint	Download and fill in the complaint form and send it to the address on the form. Complaint must be sent within three (3) months of the test date. Response will be within twenty (20) working days.

ABOUT THE BOOK

This Life in the UK Test Made Easy 3rd Edition book contains all you need to know to pass the Life in the UK Test. With you and new residents in mind, Blesilda Zarate-Robb has come up with this latest version. This is based on the official publication by the TSO, the Life in the United Kingdom - A Guide for New Residents 3rd Edition and apart from this copyrighted material, everything here - layout, design, cover, photos - is hers and separately copyrighted.

The writing of her book came about when she was due to take the Life in the UK Test herself.
Reading through the official guide, page by page, she ended up writing her own notes for easy revision.
Later on at the Home Office, when she was asked, 'Do you know your score?' She replied, 'I have no idea'.
She was told, 'You only made one mistake.' That made her day! She felt she must have done something right.
She thought why not share it - thus came her own version - 'Life in the UK Test Made Easy' based on the
Life in the United Kingdom - A Journey to Citizenship 2nd Edition.

The gaining popularity of the Life in the UK Test itself, and the growing number of people taking it, inspired her to do a new, updated version. This latest book is the result. This Life in the UK Test Made Easy 3rd Edition has been designed to make your Life in the UK Test easier for you.

A WORD FROM THE AUTHOR

Congratulations, you made a good decision to come to the UK.
For whatever purpose, whether you have come to visit, to study or to work - the UK welcomes you!

I did not have specific expectations nor impressions when I first came to the UK. As I went along as a migrant, I learnt, I adapted, I changed. I eventually made an important decision to become a permanent part of British society, and among the many decisions I have made in my life, this one is good - this one is lasting.

You might be thinking of making the same decision too.
If you are here temporarily and considering a permanent stay, this book is useful for you.
You can find out more information by visiting the website : www.gov.uk

I wish you good luck in your new life here in the UK.
Remember, life in the UK is more than just a test - it is a journey, so live it!

THE LIFE IN THE UK TEST

THE VALUES AND PRINCIPLES OF THE UK
BECOMING A PERMANENT RESIDENT
TAKING THE LIFE IN THE UK TEST
HOW TO USE THIS HANDBOOK
WHERE TO FIND MORE INFORMATION

CHECK THAT YOU UNDERSTAND
The origin of the values underlying British society
The fundamental principles of British life
The responsibilities and freedoms which come with permanent residence
The process of becoming a permanent resident or citizen

THE VALUES AND PRINCIPLES OF THE UK

Britain is a fantastic place to live : a modern, thriving society with a long and illustrious history.
Our people have been at the heart of the world's political, scientific, industrial and cultural development.
We are proud of our record of welcoming new migrants who will add to the diversity and dynamism
of our national life.

- British society is founded on fundamental values and principles which all those living in the UK
  should respect and support. These values are reflected in the :
  responsibilities, rights and privileges of being a British citizen or permanent resident of the UK.
  They are based on history and traditions and are protected by law, customs and expectations.
  There is no place in British society for extremism or intolerance.

- The fundamental principles of British life include :
  Democracy
  The rule of law
  Individual liberty
  Tolerance of those with different faiths and beliefs
  Participation in community life.

- As part of the citizenship ceremony, new citizens pledge to uphold these values.
  Flowing from the fundamental principles are 'responsibilities and freedoms' -
  which are shared by all those living in the UK and which we expect all residents to respect.

- If you wish to be a permanent resident or citizen of the UK, you should :
  respect and obey the law
  respect the rights of others, including their right to their own opinions
  treat others with fairness
  look after yourself and your family
  look after the area in which you live and the environment.

- In return, the UK offers :
  freedom of belief and religion
  freedom of speech
  freedom from unfair discrimination
  a right to a fair trial
  a right to join in the election of a government.

BECOMING A PERMANENT RESIDENT

Applying to become a permanent resident or citizen of the UK is an important decision and commitment. You will be agreeing to accept the responsibilities which go with permanent residence and to respect the laws, values and traditions of the UK. Good citizens are an asset to the UK. We welcome those seeking to make a positive contribution to our society.

- To apply to become a permanent resident or citizen of the UK, you will need to :
  speak and read English, have a good understanding of life in the UK.

- As of January 2013, there are currently two (2) ways you can be tested on these requirements :

  Take the Life in the UK Test
  The questions are written in a way that requires an understanding of the English Language at English for Speakers of Other Languages (ESOL) Entry Level 3, so there is no need to take a separate English Language Test. People here on work visas, including those on Tier 1 and Tier 2 of the points-based system, normally must pass the Life in the UK Test to become permanent residents.

  Pass an ESOL course in English with Citizenship
  You will need to take this course if your standard of English is below ESOL Entry Level 3.
  The course will help you to improve your English and learn more about Life in the UK.
  At the end of the course you will take a test.

  Once you have passed one of these tests, you can make an application for permanent residence or British citizenship. The form that you have to complete and the evidence that you need to provide will depend on your personal circumstances. There is a fee for submitting an application, which is different for the various types of application. All of the forms and a list of fees can be found on the UK Border Agency website : www.ukba.homeoffice.gov.uk

- From October 2013, the requirements will change.
  From that date, for permanent residence or British citizenship, you will need to :
  Pass the Life in the UK Test and Produce acceptable evidence of speaking and listening skills in English at B1 of the Common European Framework of Reference. This is equivalent to ESOL Entry Level 3.

- The requirements for citizenship applications may change in the future.
  Further details will be published on the UK Border Agency website : www.ukba.homeoffice.gov.uk and you should check the information on the website for current requirements before applying for settlement or citizenship.

TAKING THE LIFE IN THE UK TEST

Passing the Life in the UK Test is part of demonstrating that you are ready to become a permanent migrant to the UK. This handbook is designed to support you in your preparation. It will help you to integrate into society and play a full role in your local community. It will also help ensure that you have a broad general knowledge of the culture, laws and history of the UK.

- This handbook will help prepare you for taking the Life in the UK Test.
  The test consists of twenty-four (24) questions about important aspects of life in the UK.
  Questions are based on all parts of the handbook.
  The twenty-four (24) questions will be different for each person taking the test at that test session.

- The Life in the UK Test is usually taken in English,
  although special arrangements can be made if you wish to take it in Welsh or Scottish Gaelic.

- You can only take the test at a registered and approved Life in the UK Test centre.
  There are about sixty (60) test centres around the UK.
  You can only book your test online.
  Visit : www.lifeintheuktest.gov.uk

- You should not take your test at any other establishment as the UK Border Agency will only accept certificates from registered test centres.

- If you live on the Isle of Man or in the Channel Islands,
  there are different arrangements for taking the Life in the UK Test.

- When booking your test :
  read the instructions carefully
  make sure you enter your details correctly
  you will need to take some identification and proof of your address with you to the test -
  if you don't take these, you will not be able to take the test.

HOW TO USE THIS HANDBOOK

Everything that you will need to know to pass the Life in the UK Test is included in this handbook.

- The questions will be based on the whole book, including this introduction, so make sure you study the entire book thoroughly.

- The handbook has been written to ensure that anyone who can read English at ESOL Entry Level 3 or above should have no difficulty with the language.

- The glossary at the back of this handbook contains some key words and phrases, which you might find helpful.

- The 'Check that you Understand' points are for guidance.
  They will help you to identify particular things that you should understand.
  Just knowing the things 'highlighted' will not be enough to pass the test.

- You need to make sure that you understand everything in this book, so please read the information carefully.

WHERE TO FIND MORE INFORMATION

- The UK Border Agency
  www.ukba.homeoffice.gov.uk
  (for more information about the application process and the forms you will need to complete).

- The Life in the UK Test
  www.lifeintheuktest.gov.uk
  (for more information about the test and how to book a place to take one).

- Gov.UK
  www.gov.uk
  (for information about ESOL courses and how to find one in your area).

THE UNITED KINGDOM (UK)

CHECK THAT YOU UNDERSTAND
The different countries that make up the UK
The symbol of the union between England, Wales, Scotland and Ireland
What the Commonwealth is and its role
Other international organisations of which the UK is a member

WHAT IS THE UK?

The UK is made up of England, Scotland, Wales and Northern Ireland. The rest of Ireland is an independent country. The official name of the country is the : United Kingdom of Great Britain and Northern Ireland.
'Great Britain' refers only to England, Scotland and Wales, not to Northern Ireland.
The words 'Britain', 'British Isles' or 'British', however, are used in this book to refer to everyone in the UK.

• There are also several islands which are closely linked with the UK but are not part of it :
  the Channel Islands and the Isle of Man.
  These have their own governments and are called 'Crown dependencies'.

• There are also several British overseas territories in other parts of the world, such as :
  St Helena and the Falkland Islands.
  They are also linked to the UK but not a part of it.

• The UK is governed by the parliament sitting in Westminster. Wales, Scotland and Northern Ireland also have parliaments or assemblies of their own, with devolved powers in defined areas.

THE UNION FLAG

Although Ireland had had the same Monarch as England and Wales since Henry VIII,
it had remained a separate country. In 1801, Ireland became unified with England, Scotland and Wales after the Act of Union of 1800. This created the United Kingdom of Great Britain and Ireland.

• One symbol of this union between England, Scotland, Wales and Ireland was a new version of the official flag, the Union Flag. This is often called the 'Union Jack'. The flag combined crosses associated with England, Scotland and Ireland. It is still used today as the official flag of the UK.

• The Union Flag consists of three (3) crosses :
  The cross of St George, patron saint of England, is a red cross on a white ground.
  The cross of St Andrew, patron saint of Scotland, is a diagonal white cross on a blue ground.
  The cross of St Patrick, patron saint of Ireland, is a diagonal red cross on a white ground.
  There is also an official Welsh flag, which shows a Welsh dragon.
  The Welsh dragon does not appear on the Union Flag because, when the first Union Flag was created in 1606 from the flags of Scotland and England, the Principality of Wales was already united with England.

THE NATIONAL ANTHEM

The National Anthem of the UK is 'God Save the Queen'.
It is played at important national occasions and at events attended by the Queen or the Royal Family.
New citizens swear or affirm loyalty to the Queen as part of the citizenship ceremony. The first verse is :

'God save our gracious Queen!
Long live our noble Queen!
God save the Queen!
Send her victorious,
Happy and glorious,
Long to reign over us,
God save the Queen!'

THE PLEDGE

As part of the citizenship ceremony, new citizens pledge to uphold the values and principles of the UK.
The pledge is :
'I will give my loyalty to the United Kingdom and respect its rights and freedoms.
I will uphold its democratic values.
I will observe its laws faithfully and fulfil my duties and obligations as a British citizen.'

OATH OF ALLEGIANCE

I (name) swear by Almighty God that on becoming a British citizen,
I will be faithful and bear true allegiance to Her Majesty Queen Elizabeth the Second,
her Heirs and Successors, according to law.

AFFIRMATION OF ALLEGIANCE

I (name) do solemnly, sincerely and truly declare and affirm that on becoming a British Citizen,
I will be faithful and bear true allegiance to Her Majesty Queen Elizabeth the Second,
her Heirs and Successors, according to law.

THE UK AND INTERNATIONAL INSTITUTIONS

THE COMMONWEALTH

The Commonwealth is an association of countries that support each other and work together towards shared goals in democracy and development. Most member states were once part of the British Empire, although a few countries which were not have also joined. Membership is voluntary.

- The Queen is the ceremonial head of the Commonwealth, which currently has fifty-four (54) member states.
- The Commonwealth has no power over its members, although it can suspend membership.
- The Commonwealth is based on the : core values of democracy, good government and the rule of law.

THE COMMONWEALTH MEMBERS

Antigua and Barbuda
Australia
The Bahamas
Bangladesh
Barbados
Belize
Botswana
Brunei Darussalam
Cameroon
Canada
Cyprus
Dominica
Fiji (currently suspended)
The Gambia
Ghana
Grenada
Guyana
India

Jamaica
Kenya
Kiribati
Lesotho
Malawi
Malaysia
Maldives
Malta
Mauritius
Mozambique
Namibia
Nauru
New Zealand
Nigeria
Pakistan
Papua New Guinea
Rwanda
Samoa

Seychelles
Sierra Leone
Singapore
Solomon Islands
South Africa
Sri Lanka
St Kitts and Nevis
St Lucia
St Vincent and the Grenadines
Swaziland
Tanzania
Tonga
Trinidad and Tobago
Tuvalu
Uganda
United Kingdom (UK)
Vanuatu
Zambia

THE COUNCIL OF EUROPE

- The Council of Europe is separate from the EU.
  It has forty-seven (47) member countries, including the UK, and is responsible for the protection and promotion of human rights in those countries.

- It has no power to make laws but draws up conventions and charters, the most well-known of which is the European Convention on Human Rights and Fundamental Freedoms, usually called the European Convention on Human Rights.

THE EUROPEAN UNION

- The European Union (EU), originally called the European Economic Community (EEC), was set up by six (6) western European countries who signed the Treaty of Rome on 25 March 1957.

- The six (6) western European countries : Belgium, France, Germany, Italy, Luxembourg and the Netherlands. The UK originally decided not to join this group but it became a member in 1973. There are now twenty-seven (27) EU member states. Croatia will also become a member state in 2013.

- EU law is legally binding in the UK and all the other EU member states. European laws are called : directives, regulations or framework decisions.

THE EU MEMBER STATES

Austria	Latvia
Belgium	Lithuania
Bulgaria	Luxembourg
Cyprus	Malta
Czech Republic	Netherlands
Denmark	Poland
Estonia	Portugal
Finland	Romania
France	Slovakia
Germany	Slovenia
Greece	Spain
Hungary	Sweden
Ireland	UK
Italy	

THE UNITED NATIONS

The UK is part of the United Nations (UN), an international organisation with more than one hundred and ninety (190) countries as members.

- The UN was set up after the Second World War and aims to prevent war and promote international peace and security.

- There are fifteen (15) members on the UN Security Council, which recommends action when there are international crises and threats to peace.

- The UK is one of five (5) permanent members of the Security Council.

THE NORTH ATLANTIC TREATY ORGANIZATION (NATO)

The UK is also a member of NATO.

- NATO is a group of European and North American countries that have agreed to help each other if they come under attack.

- It also aims to maintain peace between all of its members.

A LONG AND ILLUSTRIOUS HISTORY

CHECK THAT YOU UNDERSTAND
The history of the UK before the Romans
The impact of the Romans on British society
The different groups that invaded after the Romans
The importance of the Norman invasion in 1066
The wars that took place in the Middle Ages
How Parliament began to develop
The way that land ownership worked
The effects of the Black Death
The development of English language and culture
The Wars of the Roses and the founding of the House of Tudor
How and why religion changed during this period
The importance of poetry and drama in the Elizabethan period
About the involvement of Britain in Ireland
The development of Parliament and the only period in history when England was a republic
Why there was a restoration of the monarchy
How the Glorious Revolution happened
The change in the balance of power between Parliament and the monarchy
When and why Scotland joined England and Wales to become Great Britain
The reasons for a rebellion in Scotland led by Bonnie Prince Charlie
The ideas of the Enlightenment
The importance of the Industrial Revolution and the development of industry
The slave trade and when it was abolished
The growth of the British Empire
How democracy developed during this period
What happened during the First World War
The partition of Ireland and the establishment of the UK as it is today
The events of the Second World War
The establishment of the welfare state and How life in Britain changed in the 1960s and 1970s
Events since 1979

EARLY BRITAIN

STONE AGE

- The first people to live in Britain were hunter-gatherers, in what we call the Stone Age.
  For much of the Stone Age, Britain was connected to the continent by a land bridge.
  People came and went, following herds of deer and horses which they hunted. Britain only became
  permanently separated from the continent by the Channel about ten thousand (10,000) years ago.

- The first farmers arrived in Britain six thousand (6,000) years ago.
  The ancestors of these first farmers probably came from south-east Europe.
  These people built houses, tombs and monuments on the land.

- One of these monuments, Stonehenge, still stands in what is now the English county of Wiltshire.
  Stonehenge was probably a special gathering place for seasonal ceremonies.
  Other Stone Age sites have also survived. Skara Brae on Orkney, off the north coast of Scotland,
  is the best preserved prehistoric village in northern Europe, and has helped archaeologists to understand
  more about how people lived near the end of the Stone Age.

BRONZE AGE

- Around four thousand (4,000) years ago, people learned to make bronze.
  We call this period the Bronze Age. People lived in roundhouses and buried their dead in tombs called
  round barrows. The people of the Bronze Age were accomplished metalworkers who made many
  beautiful objects in bronze and gold, including : tools, ornaments and weapons.

IRON AGE

- The Bronze Age was followed by the Iron Age, when people learned how to make weapons and tools
  out of iron. People still lived in roundhouses, grouped together into larger settlements, and sometimes
  defended sites called hill forts. A very impressive hill fort can still be seen today at Maiden Castle,
  in the English county of Dorset. Most people were farmers, craft workers or warriors.

- The language they spoke was part of the Celtic language family. Similar languages were spoken across
  Europe in the Iron Age, and related languages are still spoken today in some parts of Wales, Scotland
  and Ireland. The people of the Iron Age had a sophisticated culture and economy.
  They made the first coins to be minted in Britain, some inscribed with the names of Iron Age Kings.
  This marks the beginnings of British history.

THE ROMANS

- Julius Caesar led a Roman invasion of Britain in 55 BC. This was unsuccessful and for nearly one hundred (100) years Britain remained separate from the Roman Empire. In AD 43 the Emperor Claudius led the Roman army in a new invasion. This time, there was resistance from some of the British tribes but the Romans were successful in occupying almost all of Britain.

- One of the tribal leaders who fought against the Romans was Boudicca, the Queen of the Iceni in what is now eastern England. She is still remembered today and there is a statue of her on Westminster Bridge in London, near the Houses of Parliament.

- Areas of what is now Scotland were never conquered by the Romans, and the Emperor Hadrian built a wall in the north of England to keep out the Picts (ancestors of the Scottish people). Included in the wall were a number of forts. Parts of Hadrian's Wall, including the forts of Housesteads and Vindolanda, can still be seen. It is a popular area for walkers and is a United Nations Educational, Scientific and Cultural Organization (UNESCO) World Heritage Site.

- The Romans remained in Britain for four hundred (400) years. They built roads and public buildings, created a structure of law and introduced new plants and animals. It was during the 3rd and 4th centuries AD that the first Christian communities began to appear in Britain.

THE ANGLO-SAXONS

- The Roman army left Britain in AD 410 to defend other parts of the Roman Empire and never returned. Britain was again invaded by tribes from northern Europe : the Jutes, the Angles and the Saxons. The languages they spoke are the basis of modern-day English. Battles were fought against these invaders but, by about AD 600, the Anglo-Saxon kingdoms were established in Britain. These kingdoms were mainly in what is now England.

- The burial place of one of the kings was at Sutton Hoo in modern Suffolk. This king was buried with treasure and armour, all placed in a ship which was then covered by a mound of earth. An Anglo-Saxon helmet found at Sutton Hoo is currently on display at the British Museum. Parts of the west of Britain, including much of what is now Wales, and Scotland, remained free of Anglo-Saxon rule. The Anglo-Saxons were not Christians when they first came to Britain but, during this period, missionaries came to Britain to preach about Christianity. Missionaries from Ireland spread the religion in the north. The most famous of these were : **St Patrick,** who would become the patron saint of Ireland, and **St Columba,** who founded a monastery on the island of Iona, off the coast of what is now Scotland. **St Augustine,** who led missionaries from Rome, who spread Christianity in the south. **St Augustine** became the first Archbishop of Canterbury.

THE VIKINGS

- The Vikings came from Denmark and Norway.
  They first visited Britain in AD 789, to raid coastal towns and take away goods and slaves.
  Then, they began to stay and form their own communities in the east of England and Scotland.

- The Anglo-Saxon kingdoms in England united under King Alfred the Great, who defeated the Vikings. Many of the Viking invaders stayed in Britain - especially in the east and north of England, in an area known as the Danelaw (many place names there, such as Grimsby and Scunthorpe, come from the Viking languages). The Viking settlers mixed with local communities and some converted to Christianity.

- Anglo-Saxon kings continued to rule what is now England, except for a short period when there were Danish kings. The first of these was Cnut, also called Canute.

- In the north, the threat of attack by Vikings had encouraged the people to unite under one king, Kenneth MacAlpin. The term Scotland began to be used to describe that country.

THE NORMAN CONQUEST

- In 1066, an invasion led by William, the Duke of Normandy (in what is now northern France), defeated Harold, the Saxon King of England, at the Battle of Hastings. Harold was killed in the battle. William became king of England and is known as William the Conqueror.

- The battle is commemorated in a great piece of embroidery known as the Bayeux Tapestry, which can still be seen in France today.
  The linen cloth is nearly seventy (70) metres (230 feet) long and is embroidered with coloured wool.

- The Norman Conquest was the last successful foreign invasion of England and led to many changes in government and social structures in England. Norman French, the language of the new ruling class, influenced the development of the English language as we know it today. Initially the Normans also conquered Wales, but the Welsh gradually won territory back. The Scots and the Normans fought on the border between England and Scotland ; the Normans took over some land on the border but did not invade Scotland.

- William sent people all over England to draw up lists of all the towns and villages. The people who lived there, who owned the land and what animals they owned were also listed. This was called the Domesday Book. It still exists today and gives a picture of society in England just after the Norman Conquest.

THE MIDDLE AGES

WAR AT HOME AND ABROAD

- The period after the Norman Conquest up until about 1485 is called :
  the Middle Ages or the Medieval Period. It was a time of almost constant war.

- The English kings fought with the Welsh, Scottish and Irish noblemen for control of their lands.
  In Wales, the English were able to establish their rule.

- In 1284 King Edward I of England introduced the Statute of Rhuddlan,
  which annexed Wales to the Crown of England.
  Huge castles, including Conwy and Caernarvon, were built to maintain this power.
  By the middle of the 15th century the last Welsh rebellions had been defeated.
  English laws and the English language were introduced.

- In Scotland, the English kings were less successful. In 1314 the Scottish, led by Robert the Bruce,
  defeated the English at the Battle of Bannockburn, and Scotland remained unconquered by the English.

- At the beginning of the Middle Ages, Ireland was an independent country.
  The English first went to Ireland as troops to help the Irish king and remained to build their own
  settlements. By 1200, the English ruled an area of Ireland known as the Pale, around Dublin.
  Some of the important lords in other parts of Ireland accepted the authority of the English King.

- During the Middle Ages, the English kings also fought a number of wars abroad.
  Many knights took part in the Crusades, in which European Christians fought for control of the Holy Land.

- English kings also fought a long war with France, called the Hundred Years War,
  even though it actually lasted one hundred and sixteen (116) years.
  One of the most famous battles of the Hundred Years War was the Battle of Agincourt in 1415,
  where King Henry V's vastly outnumbered English army defeated the French.

- The English left France in the 1450s.

THE BLACK DEATH

- The Normans used a system of land ownership known as feudalism.
  The king gave land to his lords in return for help in war.
  Landowners had to send certain numbers of men to serve in the army.

- Some peasants had their own land but most were serfs.
  They had a small area of their lord's land where they could grow food.
  In return, they had to work for their lord and could not move away.

- The same system developed in southern Scotland.
  In the north of Scotland and Ireland, land was owned by members of the 'clans' (prominent families).

- In 1348, a disease, probably a form of plague, came to Britain.
  This was known as the Black Death.
  One third (1/3) of the population of England died and a similar proportion in Scotland and Wales.
  This was one of the worst disasters ever to strike Britain.

- Following the Black Death, the smaller population meant there was less need to grow cereal crops.
  There were labour shortages and peasants began to demand higher wages.

- New social classes appeared, including owners of large areas of land (later called the gentry),
  and people left the countryside to live in the towns.
  In the towns, growing wealth led to the development of a strong middle class.

- In Ireland, the Black Death killed many in the Pale and, for a time, the area controlled by the English
  became smaller.

LEGAL AND POLITICAL CHANGES

- In the Middle Ages, Parliament began to develop into the institution it is today.
  Its origins can be traced to the king's council of advisers, which included important noblemen and the leaders of the Church.

- There were few formal limits to the king's power until 1215.
  In that year, King John was forced by his noblemen to agree to a number of demands.
  The result was a charter of rights called the Magna Carta (which means the Great Charter).

- The Magna Carta established the idea that even the king was subject to the law.
  It protected the rights of the nobility and restricted the king's power to collect taxes or to make or change laws. In future, the king would need to involve his noblemen in decisions.

- In England, parliaments were called for the king to consult his nobles, particularly when the king needed to raise money. The numbers attending Parliament increased and two (2) separate parts known as Houses, were established.

- The nobility, great landowners and bishops sat in the House of Lords. Knights, who were usually smaller landowners, and wealthy people from towns and cities were elected to sit in the House of Commons.
  Only a small part of the population was able to join in electing the members of the Commons.

- A similar Parliament developed in Scotland, it had three (3) Houses, called Estates :
  the Lords, the Commons and the Clergy.

- This was also a time of development in the legal system.
  The principle that judges are independent of the government began to be established.

- In England, judges developed 'common law' by a process of precedence (that is, following previous decisions) and tradition.

- In Scotland, the legal system developed slightly differently and laws were 'codified' (that is, written down).

A DISTINCT IDENTITY

- The Middle Ages saw the development of a national culture and identity. After the Norman Conquest, the king and his noblemen had spoken Norman French and the peasants had continued to speak Anglo-Saxon. Gradually these two (2) languages combined to become one (1) English language.

- Some words in modern English are based on Norman French words - for example : 'park' and 'beauty'.
  Others are based on Anglo-Saxon words - for example : 'apple', 'cow' and 'summer'.
  In modern English, there are often two (2) words with very similar meanings - for example :
  one from French, 'demand'
  one from Anglo-Saxon, 'ask'.

- By 1400 in England, official documents were being written in English,
  and English had become the preferred language of the royal court and Parliament.

- In the years leading up to 1400, Geoffrey Chaucer wrote a series of poems in English about a group of people going to Canterbury on a pilgrimage. The people decided to tell each other stories on the journey, and the poems describe the travellers and some of the stories they told.
  This collection of poems is called 'The Canterbury Tales'.
  It was one of the first books to be printed by William Caxton,
  the first person in England to print books using a printing press.
  Many of the stories are still popular. Some have been made into plays and television programmes.

- In Scotland, many people continued to speak Gaelic and the Scots language also developed.
  A number of poets began to write in the Scots language.
  One example is John Barbour, who wrote 'The Bruce' about the Battle of Bannockburn.

- The Middle Ages also saw a change in the type of buildings in Britain.
  Castles were built in many places in Britain and Ireland, partly for defence.
  Today many are in ruins, although some, such as : Windsor and Edinburgh, are still in use.

- Great cathedrals - for example : Lincoln Cathedral - were also built, and many of these are still used for worship. Several of the cathedrals had windows of stained glass, telling stories about the Bible and Christian saints. The glass in York Minster is a famous example.

- During this period, England was an important trading nation. English wool became a very important export. People came to England from abroad to trade and also to work. Many had special skills, such as : weavers from France, engineers from Germany, glass manufacturers from Italy and canal builders from Holland.

THE WARS OF THE ROSES

- In 1455, a civil war was begun to decide who should be king of England.
  It was fought between the supporters of two (2) families :
  the House of Lancaster and the House of York.

- This war was called the Wars of the Roses, because :
  the symbol of Lancaster was a red rose and the symbol of York was a white rose.
  The war ended with the Battle of Bosworth Field in 1485.

- King Richard III of the House of York was killed in the battle and Henry Tudor,
  the leader of the House of Lancaster, became King Henry VII.
  Henry then married King Richard's niece, Elizabeth of York, and united the two (2) families.

- Henry was the first King of the House of Tudor. The symbol of the House of Tudor was a red rose with a
  white rose inside it as a sign that the Houses of York and House of Lancaster were now allies.

THE TUDORS AND STUARTS

RELIGIOUS CONFLICTS

- After his victory in the Wars of the Roses, Henry VII wanted to make sure that England remained peaceful and that his position as king was secure. He deliberately strengthened the central administration of England and reduced the power of the nobles. He was thrifty and built up the monarchy's financial reserves.
When he died, his son Henry VIII continued the policy of centralising power.
Henry VIII was King of England from 21 April 1509 until his death on 28 January 1547.
Henry VIII was most famous for : breaking away from the Church of Rome and marrying six (6) times.

- To divorce his first wife, Henry VIII needed the approval of the Pope. When the Pope refused, Henry established the Church of England. In this new Church, the king, not the Pope, would have the power to appoint bishops and order how people should worship.

- At the same time the Reformation was happening across Europe. This was a movement against the authority of the Pope and the ideas and practices of the Roman Catholic Church.
The Protestants formed their own churches : they read the Bible in their own languages instead of in Latin, they did not pray to saints or at shrines, and they believed that a person's own relationship with God was more important than submitting to the authority of the Church.

- Protestant ideas gradually gained strength in England, Wales and Scotland during the 16th century.
In Ireland, however, attempts by the English to impose Protestantism (alongside efforts to introduce the English system of laws about the inheritance of land) led to rebellion from the Irish chieftains, and much brutal fighting followed.

- During the reign of King Henry VIII, Wales became formally united with England by the Act for the Government of Wales. The Welsh sent representatives to the House of Commons and the Welsh legal system was reformed. Henry VIII was succeeded by his son Edward VI, who was strongly Protestant. During his reign, the 'Book of Common Prayer' was written to be used in the Church of England. A version of this book is still used in some churches today.

- Edward died at the age of fifteen (15) after ruling for just over six (6) years, and his half-sister Mary became queen. Mary was a devout Catholic and persecuted Protestants (for this reason, she became known as 'Bloody Mary').

- Mary also died after a short reign and the next monarch was her half-sister, Elizabeth, the daughter of Henry VIII and Anne Boleyn.

QUEEN ELIZABETH I

- Queen Elizabeth I was a Protestant.
  She re-established the Church of England as the Official Church in England.

- Everyone had to attend their local church and there were laws about the type of religious services and the prayers which could be said, but Elizabeth did not ask about people's real beliefs.
  She succeeded in finding a balance between the views of Catholics and the more extreme Protestants.
  In this way, she avoided any serious religious conflict within England.

- Elizabeth became one of the most popular monarchs in English history, particularly after 1588, when the English defeated the Spanish Armada (a large fleet of ships), which had been sent by Spain to conquer England and restore Catholicism.

THE REFORMATION IN SCOTLAND AND MARY, QUEEN OF SCOTS

- Scotland had also been strongly influenced by Protestant ideas.
  In 1560, the predominantly Protestant Scottish Parliament abolished the authority of the Pope in Scotland and Roman Catholic religious services became illegal.

- A Protestant Church of Scotland with an elected leadership was established but, unlike in England, this was not a state Church.

- The queen of Scotland, Mary Stuart (often now called 'Mary, Queen of Scots') was a Catholic.
  She was only a week old when her father died and she became queen.
  Much of her childhood was spent in France.
  When she returned to Scotland, she was the centre of a power struggle between different groups.

- When her husband was murdered, Mary was suspected of involvement and fled to England.
  She gave her throne to her Protestant son, James VI of Scotland.

- Mary was Elizabeth I's cousin and hoped that Elizabeth might help her, but Elizabeth suspected Mary of wanting to take over the English throne, and kept her a prisoner for twenty (20) years.

- Mary was eventually executed, accused of plotting against Elizabeth I.

EXPLORATION, POETRY AND DRAMA

- The Elizabethan period in England was a time of growing patriotism : a feeling of pride in being English. English explorers sought new trade routes and tried to expand British trade into the Spanish colonies in the Americas.

- Sir Francis Drake, one of the commanders in the defeat of the Spanish Armada, was one of the founders of England's naval tradition. His ship the 'Golden Hind', was one of the first to sail right around ('circumnavigate') the world.

- In Elizabeth I's time, English settlers first began to colonise the eastern coast of America. This colonisation, particularly by people who disagreed with the religious views of the next two (2) kings, greatly increased in the next century.

- The Elizabethan period is also remembered for the richness of its poetry and drama, especially the plays and poems of William Shakespeare.

JAMES VI AND I

- Elizabeth I never married and so had no children of her own to inherit her throne. When she died in 1603, her heir was her cousin James VI of Scotland. He became King James I of England, Wales and Ireland but Scotland remained a separate country.

THE KING JAMES BIBLE

- One achievement of King James' reign was a new translation of the Bible into English. This translation is known as the : 'King James Version' or the 'Authorised Version'

- It was not the first English Bible but is a version which continues to be used in many Protestant churches today.

IRELAND

- During this period, Ireland was an almost completely Catholic country.
  Henry VII and Henry VIII had extended English control outside the Pale and had established English authority over the whole country. Henry VIII took the title 'King of Ireland'.

- English laws were introduced and local leaders were expected to follow the instructions of the Lord Lieutenants in Dublin.

- During the reigns of Elizabeth I and James I, many people in Ireland opposed rule by the Protestant government in England. There were a number of rebellions.

- The English government encouraged Scottish and English Protestants to settle in Ulster, the northern province of Ireland, taking over the land from Catholic landholders.
  These settlements were known as plantations.

- Many of the new settlers came from south-west Scotland and other land was given to companies based in London. James later organised similar plantations in several other parts of Ireland.
  This had serious long-term consequences for the history of England, Scotland and Ireland.

THE RISE OF PARLIAMENT

- Elizabeth I was very skilled at managing Parliament.
  During her reign, she was successful in balancing her wishes and views against those of the House of Lords and those of the House of Commons, which was increasingly Protestant in its views.

- James I and his son Charles I were less skilled politically.
  Both believed in the 'Divine Right of Kings' : the idea that the king was directly appointed by God to rule.
  They thought that the king should be able to act without having to seek approval from Parliament.
  When Charles I inherited the thrones of England, Wales, Ireland and Scotland, he tried to rule in line with this principle. When he could not get Parliament to agree with his religious and foreign policies, he tried to rule without Parliament at all.

- For eleven (11) years, he found ways in which to raise money without Parliament's approval but eventually trouble in Scotland meant that he had to recall Parliament.

THE BEGINNING OF THE ENGLISH CIVIL WAR

- Charles I wanted the worship of the Church of England to include more ceremony and introduced a revised Prayer Book. He tried to impose this Prayer Book on the Presbyterian Church in Scotland and this led to serious unrest.

- A Scottish army was formed and Charles could not find the money he needed for his own army without the help of Parliament. In 1640, he recalled Parliament to ask it for funds.

- Many in Parliament were Puritans,
  a group of Protestants who advocated strict and simple religious doctrine and worship.
  They did not agree with the king's religious views and disliked his reforms of the Church of England.
  Parliament refused to give the king the money he asked for, even after the Scottish army invaded England.

- Another rebellion began in Ireland because the Roman Catholics in Ireland were afraid of the growing power of the Puritans. Parliament took this opportunity to demand control of the English army -
  a change that would have transferred substantial power from the king to Parliament.

- In response, Charles I entered the House of Commons and tried to arrest five (5) parliamentary leaders, but they had been warned and were not there. (No monarch has set foot in the Commons since).
  Civil war between the king and Parliament could not now be avoided and began in 1642.

- The country split into :
  those who supported the king (the Cavaliers), and
  those who supported Parliament (the Roundheads).

OLIVER CROMWELL AND THE ENGLISH REPUBLIC

- The king's army was defeated at the Battles of Marston Moor and Naseby.
  By 1646, it was clear that Parliament had won the war.
  Charles was held prisoner by the Parliamentary army.
  He was still unwilling to reach any agreement with Parliament and in 1649 he was executed.

- England declared itself a republic, called the Commonwealth.
  It no longer had a monarch.
  For a time, it was not totally clear how the country would be governed.
  For now, the army was in control.

- One of its generals, Oliver Cromwell, was sent to Ireland, where the revolt which had begun in 1641 still continued and where there was still a Royalist army.

- Cromwell was successful in establishing the authority of the English Parliament but did this with such violence that even today Cromwell remains a controversial figure in Ireland.

- The Scots had not agreed to the execution of Charles I and declared his son Charles II to be king.
  He was crowned king of Scotland and led a Scottish army into England.
  Cromwell defeated this army in the Battles of Dunbar and Worcester. Charles II escaped from Worcester, famously hiding in an oak tree on one occasion, and eventually fled to Europe.
  Parliament now controlled Scotland as well as England and Wales.

- After his campaign in Ireland and victory over Charles II at Worcester,
  Cromwell was recognised as the leader of the new republic.
  He was given the title of Lord Protector and ruled until his death in 1658.

- When Cromwell died, his son, Richard, became Lord Protector in his place but was not able to control the army or the government.

- Although Britain had been a republic for eleven (11) years,
  without Oliver Cromwell there was no clear leader or system of government.
  Many people in the country wanted stability. People began to talk about the need for a king.

THE RESTORATION

- In May 1660, Parliament invited Charles II to come back from exile in the Netherlands.
  He was crowned King Charles II of England, Wales, Scotland and Ireland. Charles II made it clear that he had 'no wish to go on his travels again'. He understood that he could not always do as he wished but would sometimes need to reach agreement with Parliament.

- Generally, Parliament supported his policies. The Church of England again became the established official Church. Both Roman Catholics and Puritans were kept out of power.

- During Charles II's reign, in 1665, there was a major outbreak of plague in London.
  Thousands of people died, especially in poorer areas. The following year,
  a great fire destroyed much of the city, including many churches and St Paul's Cathedral.
  London was rebuilt with a new St Paul's, which was designed by a famous architect, Sir Christopher Wren.
  Samuel Pepys wrote about these events in a diary which was later published and is still read today.

- The Habeas Corpus Act, became law in 1679. This was a very important piece of legislation which remains relevant today. Habeas corpus is Latin for 'you must present the person in court'. The Act guaranteed that no one could be held prisoner unlawfully. Every prisoner has a right to a court hearing.

- Charles II was interested in science. During his reign, the Royal Society was formed to promote 'natural knowledge'. This is the oldest surviving scientific society in the world.
  Among its early members were : Sir Isaac Newton and Edmund Halley (who successfully predicted the return of the comet now called Halley's Comet).

A CATHOLIC KING

- Charles II had no legitimate children. He died in 1685 and his brother, James who was a Roman Catholic, became : King James II in England, Wales and Ireland and King James VII of Scotland.

- James favoured Roman Catholics and allowed them to be army officers, which an Act of Parliament had forbidden. He did not seek to reach agreements with Parliament and arrested some of the bishops of the Church of England. People in England worried that James wanted to make England a Catholic country once more.

- However, his heirs were his two (2) daughters, who were both firmly Protestant, and people thought that this meant there would soon be a Protestant monarch again. Then, James's wife had a son.
  Suddenly, it seemed likely that the next monarch would not be a Protestant after all.

THE GLORIOUS REVOLUTION

- James II's elder daughter, Mary, was married to her cousin William of Orange,
  the Protestant ruler of the Netherlands.

- In 1688, important Protestants in England asked William to invade England and proclaim himself king.
  When William reached England, there was no resistance.
  James fled to France and William took over the throne, becoming :
  William III in England, Wales and Ireland, and William II of Scotland.

- William ruled jointly with Mary. This event was later called the 'Glorious Revolution' because
  there was no fighting in England and because it guaranteed the power of Parliament,
  ending the threat of a monarch ruling on his or her own as he or she wished.

- James II wanted to regain the throne and invaded Ireland with the help of a French army.
  William defeated James II at the Battle of the Boyne in Ireland in 1690,
  an event which is still celebrated by some in Northern Ireland today.

- William re-conquered Ireland and James fled back to France. Many restrictions were placed on the Roman
  Catholic Church in Ireland and Irish Catholics were unable to take part in the government.

- There was also support for James in Scotland.
  An attempt at an armed rebellion in support of James was quickly defeated at Killiecrankie.
  All Scottish clans were required formally to accept William as king by taking an oath.
  The MacDonalds of Glencoe were late in taking the oath and were all killed.
  The memory of this massacre meant some Scots distrusted the new government.

- Some continued to believe that James was the rightful king, particularly in Scotland.
  Some joined him in exile in France ; others were secret supporters.
  James's supporters became known as Jacobites.

A GLOBAL POWER

CONSTITUTIONAL MONARCHY - THE BILL OF RIGHTS

- At the coronation of William and Mary, a Declaration of Rights was read.
  This confirmed that the king would no longer be able to raise taxes or administer justice without agreement from Parliament. The balance of power between monarch and Parliament had now permanently changed.

- The Bill of Rights, 1689, confirmed the rights of Parliament and the limits of the king's power.
  Parliament took control of who could be monarch and declared that the king or queen must be a Protestant.

- A new Parliament had to be elected at least every three (3) years,
  later this became seven (7) years and now it is five (5) years.
  Every year the monarch had to ask Parliament to renew funding for the army and the navy.

- These changes meant that, to be able to govern effectively, the monarch needed to have advisers,
  or ministers, who would be able to ensure a majority of votes in the House of Commons and the House of Lords. There were two (2) main groups in Parliament, known as : the Whigs and the Tories.
  The modern Conservative Party is still sometimes referred to as the Tories.
  This was the beginning of party politics.

- This was also an important time for the development of a free press (newspapers and other publications which are not controlled by the government). From 1695, newspapers were allowed to operate without a government licence. Increasing numbers of newspapers began to be published.

- The laws passed after the Glorious Revolution are the beginning of what is called 'constitutional monarchy'. The monarch remained very important but was no longer able to insist on particular policies or actions if Parliament did not agree.

- After William III, the ministers gradually became more important than the monarch but this was not a democracy in the modern sense. The number of people who had the right to vote for members of Parliament was still very small. Only men who owned property of a certain value were able to vote.
  No women at all had the vote. Some constituencies were controlled by a single wealthy family.
  These were called 'pocket boroughs'.
  Other constituencies had hardly any voters and were called 'rotten boroughs'.

A GROWING POPULATION

- This was a time when many people left Britain and Ireland to settle in new colonies in America and elsewhere, but others came to live in Britain.

- The first Jews to come to Britain since the Middle Ages settled in London in 1656.
  Between 1680 and 1720 many refugees called Huguenots came from France.
  They were Protestants and had been persecuted for their religion.
  Many were educated and skilled and worked as : scientists, in banking, or in weaving or other crafts.

THE ACT OR TREATY OF UNION IN SCOTLAND

- William and Mary's successor, Queen Anne, had no surviving children.
  This created uncertainty over the succession in England, Wales and Ireland and in Scotland.

- The Act of Union, known as the Treaty of Union in Scotland, was therefore agreed in 1707, creating the Kingdom of Great Britain.

- Although Scotland was no longer an independent country, it kept its own legal and education systems and Presbyterian Church.

THE PRIME MINISTER

- When Queen Anne died in 1714, Parliament chose a German, George I to be the next King, because he was Anne's nearest Protestant relative.

- An attempt by Scottish Jacobites to put James II's son on the throne instead was quickly defeated. George I did not speak very good English and this increased his need to rely on his ministers.

- The most important minister in Parliament became known as the Prime Minister.

- The first man to be called this was Sir Robert Walpole, who was Prime Minister from 1721 to 1742.

THE REBELLION OF THE CLANS

- In 1745 there was another attempt to put a Stuart king back on the throne in place of George I's son, George II.

- Charles Edward Stuart (Bonnie Prince Charlie), the grandson of James II, landed in Scotland.
  He was supported by clansmen from the Scottish highlands and raised an army.
  Charles initially had some successes but was defeated by George II's army at the Battle of Culloden in 1746. Charles escaped back to Europe.

- The clans lost a lot of their power and influence after Culloden.
  Chieftains became landlords if they had the favour of the English king,
  and clansmen became tenants who had to pay for the land they used.

- A process began which became known as the 'Highland Clearances'.
  Many Scottish landlords destroyed individual small farms (known as 'crofts') to make space for large flocks of sheep and cattle. Evictions became very common in the early 19th century.
  Many Scottish people left for North America at this time.

THE ENLIGHTENMENT

- During the 18th century, new ideas about politics, philosophy and science were developed.
  This is often called 'the Enlightenment'.

- Many of the great thinkers of the Enlightenment were Scottish.
  Adam Smith developed ideas about economics which are still referred to today.

- David Hume's ideas about human nature continue to influence philosophers.

- Scientific discoveries, such as James Watt's work on steam power, helped the progress of the Industrial Revolution.

- One of the most important principles of the 'Enlightenment' was that everyone should have the right to their own political and religious beliefs and that the state should not try to dictate to them.
  This continues to be an important principle in the UK today.

THE INDUSTRIAL REVOLUTION

- Before the 18th century, agriculture was the biggest source of employment in Britain. There were many cottage industries, where people worked from home to produce goods such as : cloth and lace.

- The Industrial Revolution was the rapid development of industry in Britain in the 18th and 19th centuries. Britain was the first country to industrialise on a large scale.
It happened because of the development of machinery and the use of steam power.
Agriculture and the manufacturing of goods became mechanised.
This made things more efficient, and increased production.

- Coal and other raw materials were needed to power the new factories.
Many people moved from the countryside and started working in the mining and manufacturing industries.

- The development of the Bessemer process for the mass production of steel led to the development of the shipbuilding industry and the railways. Manufacturing jobs became the main source of employment in Britain.

- Better transport links were needed to transport raw materials and manufactured goods.
Canals were built to link the factories to towns and cities and to the ports,
particularly in the new industrial areas in the middle and north of England.

- Working conditions during the Industrial Revolution were very poor.
There were no laws to protect employees, who were often forced to work long hours in dangerous situations. Children also worked and were treated in the same way as adults.
Sometimes they were treated even more harshly.

- This was also a time of increased colonisation overseas.
Captain James Cook mapped the coast of Australia and a few colonies were established there.
Britain gained control over Canada, and the East India Company, originally set up to trade,
gained control of large parts of India. Colonies began to be established in southern Africa.

- Britain traded all over the world and began to import more goods.
Sugar and tobacco came from North America and the West Indies ;
textiles, tea and spices came from India and the area that is today called Indonesia.

- Trading and settlements overseas sometimes brought Britain into conflict with other countries, particularly France, which was expanding and trading in a similar way in many of the same areas of the world.

THE SLAVE TRADE

- This commercial expansion and prosperity was sustained in part by the booming slave trade.
  While slavery was illegal within Britain itself, by the 18th century it was a fully established overseas industry, dominated by Britain and the American colonies.

- Slaves came primarily from West Africa. Travelling on British ships in horrible conditions,
  they were taken to America and the Caribbean, where they were made to work on :
  tobacco and sugar plantations.

- The living and working conditions for slaves were very bad.
  Many slaves tried to escape and others revolted against their owners in protest at their terrible treatment.

- There were, however, people in Britain who opposed the slave trade.
  The first formal anti-slavery groups were set up by the Quakers in the late 1700s, and they petitioned Parliament to ban the practice.

- William Wilberforce, an evangelical Christian and a member of Parliament, also played an important part in changing the law. Along with other abolitionists (people who supported the abolition of slavery), he succeeded in turning public opinion against the slave trade.

- In 1807, it became illegal to trade slaves in British ships or from British ports,
  and in 1833 the Emancipation Act abolished slavery throughout the British Empire.

- The Royal Navy stopped slave ships from other countries, freed the slaves and punished the slave traders.

- After 1833, two (2) million Indian and Chinese workers were employed to replaced the freed slaves.
  They worked on sugar plantations in the Caribbean, in mines in South Africa, on railways in East Africa and in the army in Kenya.

THE AMERICAN WAR OF INDEPENDENCE

- By the 1760s, there were substantial British colonies in North America.
  The colonies were wealthy and largely in control of their own affairs.
  Many of the colonist families had originally gone to North America in order to have religious freedom.
  They were well educated and interested in ideas of liberty.

- The British government wanted to tax the colonies.
  The colonists saw this as an attack on their freedom and said there should be 'no taxation without representation' in the British Parliament. Parliament tried to compromise by repealing some of the taxes, but relationships between the British government and the colonies continued to worsen.
  Fighting broke out between the colonists and the British forces.

- In 1776, thirteen (13) American colonies declared their independence, stating that people had a right to establish their own governments. The colonists eventually defeated the British army and the Britain recognised the colonies' independence in 1783.

WAR WITH FRANCE

- During the 18th century, Britain fought a number of wars with France.
  In 1789, there was a revolution in France and the new French government soon declared war on Britain.
  Napoleon, who became Emperor of France, continued the war.

- Britain's navy fought against combined French and Spanish fleets, winning the Battle of Trafalgar in 1805.
  Admiral Nelson was in charge of the British fleet at Trafalgar and was killed in the battle.
  Nelson's Column in Trafalgar Square, London, is a monument to him.
  His ship, HMS Victory, can be visited in Portsmouth.

- The British army also fought against the French.
  In 1815, the French Wars ended with the defeat of the Emperor Napoleon by the Duke of Wellington at the Battle of Waterloo. Wellington was known as the 'Iron Duke' and later became Prime Minister.

- The Battle of Trafalgar, 21 October 1805 was a naval engagement fought by the British Royal Navy against the combined fleets of the French Navy and Spanish Navy.

THE VICTORIAN AGE

- In 1837, Queen Victoria became queen of the UK at the age of eighteen (18).
  She reigned until 1901, for almost sixty-four (64) years.

- At the date of writing (2013) this is the longest reign of any British monarch.
  Her reign is known as the Victorian Age.
  It was a time when Britain increased in power and influence abroad.

- Within the UK, the middle classes became increasingly significant and a number of reformers led moves to improve conditions of life for the poor.

THE BRITISH EMPIRE

- During the Victorian period, the British Empire grew to cover all of India, Australia and large parts of Africa. It became the largest empire the world has ever seen, with an estimated population of more than four hundred (400) million people.

- Many people were encouraged to leave the UK to settle overseas.
  Between 1853 and 1913, as many as thirteen (13) million British citizens left the country.

- People continued to come to Britain from other parts of the world - for example :
  between 1870 and 1914, around one hundred and twenty thousand (120,000) Russian and Polish Jews came to Britain to escape persecution.

- Many settled in London's East End and in Manchester and Leeds.
  People from the Empire, including India and Africa, also came to Britain to : live, work and study.

TRADE AND INDUSTRY

- Britain continued to be a great trading nation.

- The government began to promote policies of free trade, abolishing a number of taxes on imported goods.
  One example of this was : the repealing of the Corn Laws in 1846.
  These had prevented the import of cheap grain. The reforms helped the development of British industry,
  because raw materials could now be imported more cheaply.

- Working conditions in factories gradually became better.

- In 1847, the number of hours that women and children could work was limited by law to ten (10) hours
  per day. Better housing began to be built for workers.

- Transport links also improved, enabling goods and people to move more easily around the country.
  Just before Victoria came to the throne, the father and son George and Robert Stephenson pioneered the
  railway engine and a major expansion of the railways took place in the Victorian period.
  Railways were built throughout the Empire. There were also great advances in other areas,
  such as the building of bridges by engineers such as : Isambard Kingdom Brunel.

- British industry led the world in the 19th century.
  The UK produced more than half of the world's iron, coal and cotton cloth.
  The UK also became a centre for financial services, including insurance and banking.

- In 1851, the Great Exhibition opened in Hyde Park in the Crystal Palace,
  a huge building made of iron and glass. Exhibits ranged from huge machines to handmade goods.
  Countries from all over the world showed their goods but most of the objects were made in Britain.

THE CRIMEAN WAR

- From 1853 to 1856, Britain fought with Turkey and France against Russia in the Crimean War.
  It was the first war to be extensively covered by the media through news stories and photographs.
  The conditions were very poor and many soldiers died from illnesses they caught in the hospitals,
  rather than from war wounds. Queen Victoria introduced the Victoria Cross medal during this war.
  It honours acts of valour by soldiers.

IRELAND IN THE 19TH CENTURY

- Conditions in Ireland were not as good as in the rest of the UK.
  Two-thirds (2/3) of the population still depended on farming to make their living,
  often on very small plots of land. Many depended on potatoes as a large part of their diet.

- In the middle of the century the potato crop failed, and Ireland suffered a famine.
  A million people died from disease and starvation.
  Another million and a half left Ireland.
  Some emigrated to the United States and others came to England.

- By 1861, there were large populations of Irish people in cities such as :
  Liverpool, London, Manchester and Glasgow.

- The Irish Nationalist movement had grown strongly through 19th century.
  Some, such as the Fenians, favoured complete independence.
  Others, such as Charles Stuart Parnell, advocated 'Home Rule',
  in which Ireland would remain in the UK but have its own Parliament.

THE RIGHT TO VOTE

- As the middle classes in the wealthy industrial towns and cities grew in influence, they began to demand more political power.

- The Reform Act of 1832 had greatly increased the number of people with the right to vote. The Act also abolished the old pocket and rotten boroughs and more parliamentary seats were given to the towns and cities.

- There was a permanent shift of political power from the countryside to the towns but voting was still based on ownership of property. This meant that members of the working class were still unable to vote.

- A movement began to demand the vote for the working classes and other people without property. Campaigners, called the Chartists, presented petitions to Parliament. At first they seemed to be unsuccessful, but in 1867 there was another Reform Act. This created many more urban seats in Parliament and reduced the amount of property that people needed to have before they could vote. However, the majority of men still did not have the right to vote and no women could vote.

- Politicians realised that the increased number of voters meant that they needed to persuade people to vote for them if they were to be sure of being elected to Parliament. The political parties began to create organisations to reach out to ordinary voters. Universal suffrage (the right of every adult, male or female, to vote) followed in the next century.

- In common with the rest of Europe, women in 19th century Britain had fewer rights than men. Until 1870, when a woman got married, her earnings, property and money automatically belonged to her husband. Acts of Parliament in 1870 and 1882 gave wives the right to keep their own earnings and property.

- In the late 19th and early 20th centuries, an increasing number of women campaigned and demonstrated for greater rights and, in particular, the right to vote. They formed the women's suffrage movement and became known as 'suffragettes'.

THE FUTURE OF THE EMPIRE

- Although the British Empire continued to grow until the 1920s,
  there was already discussion in the late 19th century about its future direction.
  Supporters of expansion believed that the Empire benefited Britain through increased trade and commerce.

- Others thought the Empire had become over-expanded and that the frequent conflicts in many parts of the
  Empire, such as India's north-west frontier or southern Africa, were a drain on resources.
  Yet the great majority of British people believed in the Empire as a force for good in the world.

- The Boer War of 1899 to 1902 made the discussions about the future of the Empire more urgent.
  The British went to war in South Africa with settlers from the Netherlands called the Boers.
  The Boers fought fiercely and the war went on for over three (3) years.
  Many died in the fighting and many more from disease.
  There was some public sympathy for the Boers and people began to question whether the Empire could
  continue.

- As different parts of the Empire developed, they won greater freedom and autonomy from Britain.
  Eventually, by the second half of the 20th century, there was, for the most part, an orderly transition from
  Empire to Commonwealth, with countries being granted their independence.

THE 20TH CENTURY

THE FIRST WORLD WAR

- The early 20th century was a time of optimism in Britain. The nation, with its expansive Empire, well-admired navy, thriving industry and strong political institutions - was what is now known as a global 'superpower'. It was also a time of social progress. Financial help for the unemployed, old-age pensions and free school meals were just a few of the important measures introduced.

- Various laws were passed to improve safety in the workplace ; town planning rules were tightened to prevent the further development of slums ; and better support was given to mothers and their children after divorce or separation. Local government became more democratic and a salary for members of Parliament (MPs) was introduced for the first time, making it easier for more people to take part in public life.

- This era of optimism and progress was cut short when war broke out between several European nations. On 28 June 1914, Archduke Franz Ferdinand of Austria was assassinated. This set off a chain of events leading to the First World War (1914-18).

- But while the assassination provided the trigger for war, other factors such as : a growing sense of nationalism in many European states ; increasing militarism ; imperialism ; and the division of the major European powers into two (2) camps - all set the conditions for war.

- The conflict was centred in Europe, but it was a global war involving nations from around the world. Britain was part of the Allied Powers, which included (amongst others) France, Russia, Japan, Belgium, Serbia - and later, Greece, Italy, Romania and the United States.

- The whole of the British Empire was involved in the conflict - for example : more than a million Indians fought on behalf of Britain in lots of different countries, and around forty thousand (40,000) were killed.

- Also fought with the British were men from the : West Indies, Africa, Australia, New Zealand and Canada. The Allies fought against the Central Powers - mainly : Germany, the Austro-Hungarian Empire, the Ottoman Empire and later Bulgaria.

- Millions of people were killed or wounded, with more than two (2) million British casualties. One battle, the British attack on the Somme in July 1916, resulted in about sixty thousand (60,000) British casualties on the first day alone. The First World War ended at 11.00 am on 11th November 1918 with victory for Britain and its allies.

THE PARTITION OF IRELAND

- In 1913, the British government promised 'Home Rule' for Ireland.
  The proposal was to have a self-governing Ireland with its own parliament but still part of the UK.
  A 'Home Rule Bill' was introduced in Parliament.
  It was opposed by the Protestants in the north of Ireland, who threatened to resist Home Rule by force.

- The outbreak of the First World War led the British government to postpone any changes in Ireland.
  Irish Nationalists were not willing to wait and in 1916 there was an uprising (the Easter rising) against the British in Dublin. The leaders of the uprising were executed under military law.

- A guerrilla war against the British army and the police in Ireland followed.
  In 1921 a peace treaty was signed and in 1922 Ireland became two (2) countries.
  The six (6) counties in the north which were mainly Protestant remained part of the UK under the name Northern Ireland. The rest of Ireland became the Irish Free State.
  It had its own government and became a Republic in 1949.

- There were people in both parts of Ireland who disagreed with the split between the North and the South.
  They still wanted Ireland to be one independent country.
  Years of disagreement led to a terror campaign in Northern Ireland and elsewhere.
  The conflict between those wishing for full Irish independence and those wishing to remain loyal to the British government is often referred to as 'the Troubles'.

THE INTER-WAR PERIOD

- In the 1920s, many people's living conditions got better.
  There were improvements in public housing and new homes were built in many towns and cities.

- However, in 1929, the world entered the 'Great Depression' and some parts of the UK suffered mass unemployment. The effects of the depression of the 1930s were felt differently in different parts of the UK.
  The traditional heavy industries such as : shipbuilding were badly affected but new industries - including the automobile and aviation industries - developed.
  As prices generally fell, those in work had more money to spend.
  Car ownership doubled from one (1) million to two (2) million between 1930 and 1939.

- In addition, many new houses were built. It was also a time of cultural blossoming, with writers such as : Graham Greene and Evelyn Waugh prominent.
  The economist John Maynard Keynes published influential new theories of economics.
  The BBC started radio broadcasts in 1922 and began the world's first regular television service in 1936.

THE SECOND WORLD WAR

- Adolf Hitler came to power in Germany in 1933.
  He believed that the conditions imposed on Germany by the Allies after the First World War were unfair.
  He also wanted to conquer more land for the German people. He set about renegotiating treaties,
  building up arms, and testing Germany's military strength in nearby countries.

- The British government tried to avoid another war. However, when Hitler invaded Poland in 1939,
  Britain and France declared war in order to stop his aggression.

- The war was initially fought between the Axis powers (fascist Germany and Italy and the Empire of Japan)
  and the Allies. The main countries on the allied side were the :
  UK, France, Poland, Australia, New Zealand, Canada, and the Union of South Africa.

- Having occupied Austria and invaded Czechoslovakia,
  Hitler followed his invasion of Poland by taking control of Belgium and the Netherlands.
  Then, in 1940, German forces defeated allied troops and advanced through France.
  At this time of national crisis, Winston Churchill became Prime Minister and Britain's war leader.

- As France fell, the British decided to evacuate British and French soldiers from France in a huge naval
  operation. Many civilian volunteers in small pleasure and fishing boats from Britain helped the Navy to
  rescue more than three hundred thousand (300,000) men from the beaches around Dunkirk.
  Although many lives and a lot of equipment were lost, the evacuation was a success and meant that Britain
  was better able to continue the fight against the Germans.
  The evacuation gave rise to the phrase 'Dunkirk Spirit'.

- From the end of June 1940 until the German invasion of the Soviet Union in June 1941,
  Britain and the Empire stood almost alone against Nazi Germany.

- Hitler wanted to invade Britain, but before sending in troops, Germany needed to control the air.
  The Germans waged an air campaign against Britain,
  but the British resisted with their fighter planes and eventually won the crucial aerial battle against the
  Germans, called 'the Battle of Britain', in the summer of 1940.

- The most important planes used by the Royal Air Force in the 'Battle of Britain' -
  which were designed and built in Britain were : the Spitfire and the Hurricane.

- Despite this crucial victory,
  the German air force was able to continue bombing London and other British cities at night-time.
  This was called the Blitz. Coventry was almost totally destroyed and a great deal of damage was done in other cities, especially in the East End of London.

- Despite the destruction, there was a strong national spirit of resistance in the UK.
  The phrase 'the Blitz Spirit' is still used today to describe Britons pulling together in the face of adversity.

- At the same time as defending Britain, the British military was fighting the Axis on many other fronts.
  In Singapore, the Japanese defeated the British and then occupied Burma, threatening India.
  The United States entered the war when the Japanese bombed its naval base at Pearl Harbour in December 1941.

- That same year, Hitler attempted the largest invasion in history by attacking the Soviet Union.
  It was a fierce conflict, with huge losses on both sides. German forces were ultimately repelled by the Soviets, and the damage they sustained proved to be a pivotal point in the war.

- The allied forces gradually gained the upper hand, winning significant victories in North Africa and Italy.
  German losses in the Soviet Union, combined with the support of the Americans,
  meant that the Allies were eventually strong enough to attack Hitler's forces in Western Europe.

- On 06 June 1944, allied forces landed in Normandy, this event is often referred to as 'D-Day'.
  Following victory on the beaches of Normandy, the Allied forces pressed on through France and eventually into Germany. The Allies comprehensively defeated Germany in May 1945.

- The war against Japan ended in August 1945 when the United States dropped its newly developed atom bombs on the Japanese cities of Hiroshima and Nagasaki. Scientists led by Ernest Rutherford, working at Manchester and then Cambridge University,
  were the first to 'split the atom' and took part in the Manhattan Project in the United States, which developed the atomic bomb. The war was finally over.

BRITAIN SINCE 1945

THE WELFARE STATE

- Although the UK had won the war, the country was exhausted economically and people wanted change. During the war, there had been significant reforms to the education system and people now looked for wider social reforms.

- In 1945, the British people elected a Labour government. The new Prime Minister was Clement Attlee, who promised to introduce the welfare state outlined in the Beveridge Report.

- In 1948, Aneurin (Nye) Bevan, the Minister for Health, led the establishment of the National Health Service (NHS), which guaranteed a minimum standard of health care for all, free at the point of use.

- A national system of benefits was also introduced to provide 'social security', so that the population would be protected from the 'cradle to the grave'.

- The government took into public ownership (nationalised) the : railways, coal mines and gas, water and electricity supplies.

- Another aspect of change was self-government for former colonies. In 1947, independence was granted to nine (9) countries, including : India, Pakistan and Ceylon (now Sri Lanka).

- Other colonies in Africa, the Caribbean and the Pacific achieved independence over the next twenty (20) years.

- The UK developed its own atomic bomb and joined the new North Atlantic Treaty Organization (NATO), an alliance of nations set up to resist the perceived threat of invasion by the Soviet Union and its allies.

- Britain had a Conservative government from 1951 to 1964. The 1950s were a period of economic recovery after the war and increasing prosperity for working people. The Prime Minister of the day, Harold Macmillan, was famous for his 'wind of change' speech about decolonisation and independence for the countries of the Empire.

MIGRATION IN POST-WAR BRITAIN

- Rebuilding Britain after the Second World War was a huge task.
  There were labour shortages and the British government encouraged workers from Ireland and other parts of Europe to come to the UK and help with the reconstruction.
  In 1948, people from the West Indies were also invited to come and work.

- During the 1950s, there was still a shortage of labour in the UK. Further immigration was therefore encouraged for economic reasons, and many industries advertised for workers from overseas - for example : centres were set up in the West Indies to recruit people to drive buses, textile and engineering firms from the north of England and the Midlands sent agents to India and Pakistan to find workers.

- For about twenty-five (25) years, people from these countries - travelled to work and settle in Britain : West Indies, India, Pakistan and (later) Bangladesh.

SOCIAL CHANGE IN THE 1960s

- The decade of the 1960s was a period of significant social change.
  It was known as 'the Swinging Sixties'. There was a growth in British fashion, cinema and popular music.
  Two (2) well-known pop music groups at the time were : The Beatles and The Rolling Stones.
  People started to become better off and many bought cars and other consumer goods.

- It was also a time when social laws were liberalised - for example :
  in relation to divorce and to abortion in England, Wales and Scotland.

- The position of women in the workplace also improved. It was quite common at the time for employers to ask women to leave their jobs when they got married, but Parliament passed new laws giving women the right to equal pay and made it illegal for employers to discriminate against women because of their gender.

- The 1960s was also a time of technological progress.
  Britain and France developed the world's only supersonic commercial airliner, Concorde.
  New styles of architecture, including high-rise buildings and the use of concrete and steel, became common.

- The number of people migrating from the : West Indies, India, Pakistan and what is now Bangladesh fell in the late 1960s because the government passed new laws to restrict immigration to Britain.
  Immigrants were required to have a strong connection to Britain through birth or ancestry.
  Even so, during the early 1970s, Britain admitted twenty-eight thousand (28,000) people of Indian origin who had been forced to leave Uganda.

PROBLEMS IN THE ECONOMY IN THE 1970s

- In late 1970s, the post-war economic boom came to an end. Prices of goods and raw materials began to rise sharply and the exchange rate between the pound and other currencies was unstable. This caused problems with the 'balance of payments' : imports of goods were valued at more than the price paid for exports.

- Many industries and services were affected by strikes and this caused problems between the trade unions and the government. People began to argue that the unions were too powerful and that their activities were harming the UK.

- The 1970s were also a time of serious unrest in Northern Ireland.
  In 1972, the Northern Ireland Parliament was suspended and Northern Ireland was directly ruled by the UK government. Some three thousand (3,000) people lost their lives in the decades after 1969 in the violence in Northern Ireland.

EUROPE AND THE COMMON MARKET

- These countries formed the European Economic Community (EEC) in 1957 :
  West Germany, France, Belgium, Italy, Luxembourg and the Netherlands.

- At first the UK did not wish to join the EEC but it eventually did so in 1973.
  The UK is a full member of the European Union but does not use the Euro currency.

CONSERVATIVE GOVERNMENT 1979 TO 1997

- Margaret Thatcher, Britain's first woman Prime Minister, led the Conservative government from 1979 to 1990. The government made structural changes to the economy through the privatisation of nationalised industries and imposed legal controls on trade union powers.

- Deregulation saw a great increase in the role of the City of London as an international centre for :
  investments, insurance and other financial services.
  Traditional industries, such as shipbuilding and coal mining, declined.

- In 1982, Argentina invaded the Falkland Islands, a British overseas territory in the South Atlantic.
  A naval task force was sent from the UK and military action led to the recovery of the islands.

- John Major was Prime Minister after Mrs Thatcher, and helped establish the Northern Ireland peace process.

LABOUR GOVERNMENT FROM 1997 TO 2010

- In 1997 the Labour Party led by Tony Blair was elected.
  The Blair government introduced a Scottish Parliament and a Welsh Assembly.
  The Scottish Parliament has substantial powers to legislate.
  The Welsh Assembly was given fewer legislative powers but considerable control over public services.

- In Northern Ireland, the Blair government was able to build on the peace process, resulting in the Good Friday Agreement signed in 1998. The Northern Ireland Assembly was elected in 1999 but suspended in 2002. It was not reinstated until 2007. Most paramilitary groups in Northern Ireland have decommissioned their arms and are inactive. Gordon Brown took over as Prime Minister in 2007.

CONFLICTS IN AFGHANISTAN AND IRAQ

- Throughout the 1990s, Britain played a leading role in coalition forces involved in the liberation of Kuwait, following the Iraqi invasion in 1990, and the conflict in the Former Republic of Yugoslavia.

- Since 2000, British armed forces have been engaged in the global fight against international terrorism and against the proliferation of weapons of mass destruction, including operations in Afghanistan and Iraq. British combat troops left Iraq in 2009.

- The UK now operates in Afghanistan as part of the United Nations (UN) mandated fifty-nation (50 nation) International Security Assistance Force (ISAF) coalition and at the invitation of the Afghan government. ISAF is working to ensure that Afghan territory can never again be used as a safe haven for international terrorism, where groups such as Al Qa'ida could plan attacks on the international community.

- As part of this, ISAF is building up the Afghan National Security Forces and is helping to create a secure environment in which governance and development can be extended. International forces are gradually handing over responsibility for security to the Afghans, who will have full security responsibility in all provinces by the end of 2014.

COALITION GOVERNMENT 2010 ONWARDS

- In May 2010, and for the first time in the UK since February 1974, no political party won an overall majority in the General Election. The Conservative and Liberal Democrat parties formed a coalition and the leader of the Conservative Party, David Cameron, became Prime Minister.

A MODERN, THRIVING SOCIETY

CHECK THAT YOU UNDERSTAND

The capital cities of the UK
What languages other than English are spoken in particular parts of the UK
How the population of the UK has changed
That the UK is an equal society and ethnically diverse
The currency of the UK
The different religions that are practised in the UK
That the Anglican Church, also known as the Church of England,
is the Church of the state in England (the 'established Church')
That other branches of the Christian Church also practise their faith in the UK,
without being linked to the state
That other religions are practised in the UK
About the patron saints
The main Christian festivals that are celebrated in the UK
Other religious festivals that are important in the UK
Some of the other events that are celebrated in the UK
What a bank holiday is
Which sports are particularly popular in the UK
Some of the major sporting events that take place each year
Some of the major arts and culture events that happen in the UK
How achievements in arts and culture are formally recognised
Some of the ways in which people in the UK spend their leisure time
The development of British cinema
What the television licence is and how it funds the BBC
Some of the places of interest to visit in the UK

THE UK TODAY

The UK today is a more diverse society than it was one hundred (100) years ago, in both ethnic and religious terms. Post-war immigration means that nearly 10% of the population has a parent or grandparent born outside the UK. The UK continues to be a multinational and multiracial society with a rich and varied culture.

- Most people live in towns and cities but much of Britain is still countryside.
  Many people continue to visit the countryside for holidays and for leisure activities such as :
  walking, camping and fishing.

THE NATIONS OF THE UK
- UK is made up of England, Wales, Scotland and Northern Ireland.
  The UK is located in the north west of Europe. The longest distance on the mainland is from John O'Groats on the north coast of Scotland to Land's End in the south-west corner of England.
  It is about eight hundred and seventy (870) miles, approximately 1,400 kilometres.

THE CITIES OF THE UK
- The capital city of the UK is London.
- The capital city of Wales is Cardiff.
- The capital city of Scotland is Edinburgh.
- The capital city of Northern Ireland is Belfast.

ENGLAND
London
Birmingham
Liverpool
Leeds
Sheffield
Bristol
Manchester
Bradford
Newcastle Upon Tyne
Plymouth
Southampton
Norwich

WALES
Cardiff
Swansea
Newport

SCOTLAND
Edinburgh
Glasgow
Dundee
Aberdeen

NORTHERN IRELAND
Belfast

UK CURRENCY

- The currency in the UK is the pound sterling, the symbol is £.
  There are 100 pence in a pound. The denominations (values) of currency are -
  coins : 1p, 2p, 5p, 10p, 20p, 50p, £1 and £2.
  notes : £5, £10, £20, £50.

- Northern Ireland and Scotland have their own banknotes, which are valid everywhere in the UK.
  However, shops and businesses do not have to accept them.

LANGUAGES AND DIALECTS

- There are many variations in language in the different parts of the UK.
  The English language has many accents and dialects.
  In Wales, many people speak Welsh - a completely different language from English - and it is taught in
  schools and universities. In Scotland, Gaelic (again, a different language) is spoken in some parts of the
  Highlands and Islands, and in Northern Ireland, some people speak Irish Gaelic.

POPULATION

- Population growth has been faster in more recent years.
  Migration into the UK and longer life expectancy have played a part in population growth.
  The population is very unequally distributed over the four (4) parts of the UK.

- England, more or less consistently makes up 84% of the total population.
  Wales around 5%, Scotland just over 8%, and Northern Ireland less than 3%.
  The data below shows how the population of the UK has changed over time.

POPULATION GROWTH IN THE UK

Year	Population
1600	just over 4 million
1700	5 million
1801	8 million
1851	20 million
1901	40 million
1951	50 million
1998	57 million
2005	just under 60 million
2010	just over 62 million

Source : National Statistics

AN AGEING POPULATION

- People in the UK are living longer than ever before.
  This is due to improved living standards and better health care.

- There are now a record number of people aged eighty-five (85) and over.
  This has an impact on the cost of pensions and health care.

ETHNIC DIVERSITY

- The UK population is ethnically diverse and changing rapidly, especially in large cities such as London.
  It is not always easy to get an exact picture of the ethnic origin of all the population.

- There are people in the UK with ethnic origins from all over the world.
  In surveys, the most common ethnic description chosen is white, which includes people of :
  European, Australian, Canadian, New Zealand and American descent.

- Other significant groups are those of : Asian, black, and mixed descent.

AN EQUAL SOCIETY

- Within the UK, it is a legal requirement that men and women should not be discriminated against because of their gender or because they are, or are not, married.
  They have equal rights to : work, own property, marry and divorce.
  If they are married, both parents are equally responsible for their children.

- Women in Britain today make up about half (1/2) of the workforce.
  On average, girls leave school with better qualifications than boys.
  More women than men study at university.

- Employment opportunities for women are much greater than they were in the past.
  Women work in all sectors of the economy, and there are now more women in high-level positions than ever before, including senior managers in traditionally male-dominated occupations.
  Alongside this, men now work in more varied jobs than they did in the past.

- It is no longer expected that women should stay at home and not work.
  Women often continue to work after having children.
  In many families today, both partners work and both share responsibility for childcare and household chores.

RELIGION

The UK is historically a Christian country.

- In the 2009 Citizenship Survey,
  70% of people identified themselves as Christian
  4% of much smaller proportions identified themselves as Muslim
  2 % Hindu
  1% Sikh
  both less than 0.5% of Jewish or Buddhist
  2% of people followed another religion.

- There are religious buildings for other religions all over the UK.
  This includes :
  Islamic mosques
  Hindu temples
  Jewish synagogues
  Sikh gurdwaras
  Buddhist temples.

- However, everyone has the legal right to choose their religion, or to choose not to practice a religion.

- In the Citizenship Survey, 21% of people said that they had no religion.

CHRISTIAN CHURCHES

- In England, there is a constitutional link between Church and state.
  The official Church of the state is the Church of England -
  called the Anglican Church in other countries and the Episcopal Church in Scotland and the United States.
  It is a Protestant Church and has existed since the Reformation in the 1530s.

- The monarch is the head of the Church of England.
  The spiritual leader of the Church of England is the Archbishop of Canterbury.
  The monarch has the right to select the Archbishop and other senior church officials,
  but usually the choice is made by the Prime Minister and a committee appointed by the Church.
  Several Church of England bishops sit in the House of Lords.

- In Scotland, the national Church is the Church of Scotland, which is a Presbyterian Church.
  It is governed by ministers and elders. The chairperson of the General Assembly of the Church of Scotland
  is the Moderator, who is appointed for one (1) year only and often speaks on behalf of that Church.
  There is no established Church in Wales or Northern Ireland.

- Other Protestant Christian groups in the UK are : Baptists, Methodists, Presbyterians and Quakers.
  There are also other denominations of Christianity, the biggest of which is Roman Catholic.
  Westminster Abbey has been the coronation church since 1066 and is the final resting place of seventeen
  (17) monarchs.

PATRON SAINTS' DAYS

- England, Scotland, Wales and Northern Ireland each have a national saint, called a patron saint.
  Each saint has a special day :

St David's Day, Wales	01 March
St Patrick's Day, Northern Ireland	17 March
St George's Day, England	23 April
St Andrew's Day, Scotland	30 November.

- Only Scotland and Northern Ireland have their patron saint's day as an official holiday (although in
  Scotland not all businesses and offices will close). Events are held across Scotland, Northern Ireland and
  the rest of the country, especially where there are a lot of people of Scottish, Northern Irish, and Irish
  heritage. While the patron saints' days are no longer public holidays in England and Wales, they are still
  celebrated. Parades and small festivals are held all over the two (2) countries.

CUSTOMS AND TRADITIONS

THE MAIN CHRISTIAN FESTIVALS

24 December	Christmas Eve
25 December	Christmas Day
26 December	Boxing Day
March or April	Easter
40 days before Easter	Lent
Day before Lent starts	Shrove Tuesday
Lent begins on	Ash Wednesday

OTHER FESTIVALS AND TRADITIONS

31 December	Hogmanay
01 January	New Year
02 January	(is also a public holiday)
14 February	Valentine's Day
01 April	April Fool's Day
3 weeks before Easter	Mothering Sunday
3rd Sunday in June	Father's Day
31 October	Halloween
05 November	Bonfire Night
11 November	Remembrance Day

OTHER RELIGIOUS FESTIVALS

October or November	Diwali
November or December	Hannukah
Changes every year	Eid al-Fitr
	Eid ul Adha
14 April	Vaisakhi (Baisakhi)

THE MAIN CHRISTIAN FESTIVALS

- **CHRISTMAS EVE, 24 DECEMBER**
Many Christians go to church on Christmas Eve, or on Christmas Day itself.

- **CHRISTMAS DAY, 25 DECEMBER**
Celebrates the birth of Jesus Christ. It is a public holiday.
Christmas is celebrated in a traditional way.
People usually spend the day at home and eat a special meal, which often includes :
roast turkey, Christmas pudding and mince pies.
They give gifts, send cards and decorate their houses. Christmas is a special time for children.
Very young children believe that Father Christmas (also known as Santa Claus)
brings them presents during the night before Christmas Day. Many people decorate a tree in their home.

- **BOXING DAY, 26 DECEMBER**
Is the day after Christmas Day and is a public holiday.

- **EASTER, MARCH OR APRIL**
Takes place in March or April.
It marks the death of Jesus Christ on Good Friday and His rising from the dead on Easter Sunday.
Both Good Friday and the following Monday called Easter Monday, are public holidays.

- **LENT**
The forty (40) days before Easter are known as Lent.
It is a time when Christians take time to reflect and prepare for Easter. Traditionally, people would fast
during this period and today many people will give something up, like a favourite food.

- **SHROVE TUESDAY**
The day before Lent starts is called Shrove Tuesday, or Pancake Day. People eat pancakes, which were
traditionally made to use up foods such as : eggs, fat and milk before fasting.

- **ASH WEDNESDAY**
Lent begins on Ash Wednesday. There are church services where Christians are marked with an ash cross
on their forehead as a symbol of death and sorrow for sin. Easter is also celebrated by people who are not
religious. 'Easter eggs' are chocolate eggs often given as presents at Easter as a symbol of new life.

OTHER FESTIVALS AND TRADITIONS

- **HOGMANAY, 31 DECEMBER**
  In Scotland, 31 December is called Hogmanay and 02 January is also a public holiday.
  For some Scottish people, Hogmanay is a bigger holiday than Christmas.

- **NEW YEAR, 01 JANUARY**
  It is a public holiday. People usually celebrate on the night of 31 December (called New Year's Eve).

- **VALENTINE'S DAY, 14 FEBRUARY**
  It is when lovers exchange cards and gifts.
  Sometimes people send anonymous cards to someone they secretly admire.

- **APRIL FOOL'S DAY, 01 APRIL**
  It is a day when people play jokes on each other until midday.
  The television and newspapers often have stories that are April Fool jokes.

- **MOTHERING SUNDAY OR MOTHER'S DAY**
  It is the Sunday three (3) weeks before Easter. Children send cards or buy gifts for their mothers.

- **FATHER'S DAY**
  It is the third (3rd) Sunday in June. Children send cards or buy gifts for their fathers.

- **HALLOWEEN, 31 OCTOBER**
  It is an ancient festival and has roots in the pagan festival to mark the beginning of winter. Young people will often dress up in frightening costumes to play 'trick or treat'. People give them treats to stop them playing tricks on them. A lot of people carve lanterns out of pumpkins and put a candle inside.

- **BONFIRE NIGHT, 05 NOVEMBER**
  It is an occasion when people in Great Britain set off fireworks at home or in special displays.
  The origin of this celebration was an event in 1605, when a group of Catholics led by Guy Fawkes failed in their plan to kill the Protestant king with a bomb in the Houses of Parliament.

- **REMEMBRANCE DAY, 11 NOVEMBER**
  Commemorates those who died fighting for the UK and its allies. Originally it commemorated the dead of the First World War, which ended on 11 November 1918. People wear poppies (the red flower found on the battlefields of the First World War). At 11.00 am, there is a two (2)-minute silence and wreaths are laid at the Cenotaph in Whitehall, London.

OTHER RELIGIOUS FESTIVALS

- **DIWALI, OCTOBER OR NOVEMBER**
  Normally falls in October or November and lasts for five (5) days.
  It is often called the Festival of Lights. It is celebrated by Hindus and Sikhs.
  It celebrates the victory of good over evil and the gaining of knowledge.
  There are different stories about how the festival came about.
  There is a famous celebration of Diwali in Leicester.

- **HANNUKAH, NOVEMBER OR DECEMBER**
  It is celebrated for eight (8) days. It is to remember the Jews' struggle for religious freedom.
  On each day of the festival, a candle is lit on a stand of eight (8) candles (called a menorah)
  to remember the story of the festival, where oil that should have lasted only a day did so for eight (8).

- **EID AL-FITR**
  Celebrates the end of Ramadan, when Muslims have fasted for a month.
  They thank Allah for giving them the strength to complete the fast.
  The date when it takes place changes every year. Muslims attend special services and meals.

- **EID UL ADHA**
  Remembers that prophet Ibrahim was willing to sacrifice his son when God ordered him to.
  It reminds Muslims of their own commitment to God.
  Many Muslims sacrifice an animal to eat during this festival.
  In Britain this has to be done in a slaughterhouse.

- **VAISAKHI, 14 APRIL**
  Also spelled Baisakhi is a Sikh festival which celebrates the founding of the Sikh community known as the
  Khalsa. It is celebrated on 14 April each year with parades, dancing and singing.

BANK HOLIDAYS

- As well as those mentioned previously, there are other public holidays each year called bank holidays,
  when banks and many other businesses are closed for the day. These are of no religious significance.
  They are at the beginning of May, in late May or early June, and in August.
  In Northern Ireland, the anniversary of the Battle of the Boyne in July is also a public holiday.

SPORT

Sports of all kinds play an important part in many people's lives.
There are several sports that are particularly popular in the UK.

- Many sporting events take place at major stadiums such as :
  Wembley Stadium in London and the Millennium Stadium in Cardiff.

- Local governments and private companies provide sports facilities such as :
  swimming pools, tennis courts, football pitches, dry ski slopes and gymnasiums.

- Many famous sports, including : cricket, football, lawn tennis, golf and rugby, began in Britain.

- The UK has hosted the Olympic Games on three (3) occasions : 1908, 1948, 2012.
  The main Olympic site for the 2012 Games was in Stratford, East London.
  The British team was very successful, across a wide range of Olympic sports,
  finishing third (3rd) in the medal table. The Paralympic Games for 2012 were also hosted in London.

- The Paralympics have their origin in the work of Dr Sir Ludwig Guttman, a German refugee, at the Stoke
  Mandeville hospital in Buckinghamshire. Dr Guttman developed new methods of treatment for people with
  spinal injuries and encouraged patients to take part in exercise and sport.

CRICKET
- Cricket originated in England and is now played in many countries.
  Games can last up to five (5) days but still result in a draw! The idiosyncratic nature of the game and its
  complex laws are said to reflect the best of the British character and sense of fair play.
  You may come across expressions, which have passed into everyday usage such as :
  'rain stopped play'
  'batting on a sticky wicket'
  'playing a straight bat'
  'bowled a googly'
  'it's just not cricket'

- The most famous competition is the Ashes, which is a series of Test matches played between England and
  Australia.

FOOTBALL

- Football is the UK's most popular sport.
  It has a long history in the UK and the first professional football clubs were formed in the late 19th century.
  England, Wales, Scotland, and Northern Ireland each have separate leagues in which clubs representing different towns and cities compete.

- The English Premier League attracts a huge international audience.
  Many of the best players in the world play in the Premier League.
  Many UK teams also compete in competitions such as the :
  UEFA (Union of European Football Associations) Champions League, against other teams from Europe.

- Most towns and cities have a professional club and people take great pride in supporting their home team.
  There can be great rivalry between different football clubs and among fans.

- Each country in the UK also has its own national team that competes with other national teams across the world in tournaments such as :
  the FIFA (Federation Internationale de Football Association) World Cup, and
  the UEFA (European Football Championships).

- England's only international tournament victory was at the World Cup of 1966, hosted in the UK.
  Football is also a popular sport to play in many local communities,
  with people playing amateur games every week in parks all over the UK.

RUGBY

- Rugby originated in England in the early 19th century and is very popular in the UK today.

- There are two (2) different types of rugby, which have different rules : union and league.
  Both have separate leagues and national teams in England, Wales, Scotland and Northern Ireland
  (who play with the Irish Republic). Teams from all countries compete in a range of competitions.

- The most famous rugby union competition is the Six Nations Championship between :
  England, Wales, Scotland, Ireland, France and Italy.

- The Super League is the most well-known rugby league (club) competition.

HORSE RACING

- There is a very long history of horse racing in Britain,
  with evidence of events taking place as far back as Roman times.
  The sport has a long association with royalty. There are racecourses all over the UK.

- Famous horse-racing events include :
  Royal Ascot, a five-day (5 day) race meeting in Berkshire attended by members of the Royal Family ;
  the Grand National at Aintree near Liverpool ; and
  the Scottish Grand National at Ayr.
  There is a National Horseracing Museum in Newmarket, Suffolk.

GOLF

- The modern game of golf can be traced back to 15th century Scotland.
  It is a popular sport played socially as well as professionally.
  There are public and private golf courses all over the UK.

- St Andrews in Scotland is known as the home of golf.
  The Open Championship is the only 'Major' tournament held outside the United States.
  It is hosted by a different golf course every year.

TENNIS

- Modern tennis evolved in England in the late 19th century.
  The first tennis club was founded in Leamington Spa in 1872.

- The most famous tournament hosted in Britain is The Wimbledon Championships,
  which takes place each year at the All England Lawn Tennis and Croquet Club.
  It is the oldest tennis tournament in the world and the only 'Grand Slam' event played on grass.

SKIING

- Skiing is increasingly popular in the UK.
  Many people go abroad to ski and there are also dry ski slopes throughout the UK.
  Skiing on snow may also be possible during the winter.
  There are five (5) ski centres in Scotland, as well as Europe's longest dry ski slope near Edinburgh.

WATER SPORTS

- Sailing continues to be popular in the UK, reflecting our maritime heritage.
  A British sailor, Sir Francis Chichester, was the first person to sail single-handed around the world passing the Cape of Good Hope (Africa) and Cape Horn (South America), in 1966 / 1967.
  Two (2) years later, Sir Robin Knox-Johnston became the first person to do this without stopping.

- Many sailing events are held throughout the UK, the most famous of which is at Cowes on the Isle of Wight.

- Rowing is also popular, both as a leisure activity and as a competitive sport.
  There is a popular yearly race on the Thames between Oxford and Cambridge Universities.

MOTOR SPORTS

- There is a long history of motor sport in UK, for both cars and motor cycles.
  Motor-car racing in the UK started in 1902.
  The UK continues to be a world leader in the development and manufacture of motor-sport technology.

- A Formula 1 Grand Prix event is held in the UK each year and a number of British Grand Prix drivers have won the Formula 1 World Championship.
  Recent British winners include : Damon Hill, Lewis Hamilton and Jensen Button.

ARTS AND CULTURE

MUSIC

- Music is an important part of British culture, with a rich and varied heritage.
  It ranges from classical music to modern pop.
  There are many different venues and musical events that take place across the UK.

- The Proms is an eight-week (8 week) summer season of orchestral classical music
  that takes place in various venues, including the Royal Albert Hall in London.
  It has been organised by the British Broadcasting Corporation (BBC) since 1927.
  The 'Last Night of the Proms' is the most well-known concert and (along with others in the series) is
  broadcast on television. Classical music has been popular in the UK for many centuries.

- Other types of popular music, including : folk music, jazz, pop and rock music,
  have flourished in Britain since the 20th century.
  Britain has had an impact on popular music around the world, due to the wide use of the English language,
  the UK's cultural links with many countries, and British capacity for invention and innovation.

- Since the 1960s, British pop music has made one of the most important cultural contributions to life in the
  UK. Bands including : The Beatles and The Rolling Stones, continue to have an influence on music both
  here and abroad. British pop music has continued to innovate - or example :
  the Punk movement of the late 1970s, and the trend towards boy and girl bands in the 1990s.

- There are many large venues that host music events throughout the year, such as : Wembley Stadium,
  The O2 in Greenwich, south-east London and the Scottish Exhibition and Conference Centre (SECC) in
  Glasgow. Festival season takes place across the UK every summer, with major events in various locations.
  Famous festivals include : Glastonbury, the Isle of Wight Festival and the V Festival.
  Many bands and solo artists, both well-known and up-and-coming, perform at these events.

- The National Eisteddfod of Wales is an annual cultural festival which includes music, dance, art and
  original performances largely in Welsh. It includes a number of important competitions for Welsh poetry.

- The Mercury Music Prize is awarded each September for the best album from the UK and Ireland.
  The Brit Awards is an annual event that gives awards in a range of categories, such as :
  best British group and best British solo artist.

THEATRE

- There are theatres in most towns and cities throughout the UK, ranging from the large to the small.
  They are an important part of local communities and often show both professional and amateur productions.

- London's West End, also known as 'Theatreland', is particularly well known.
  The Mousetrap, a murder-mystery play by Dame Agatha Christie, has been running in the West End since 1952 and has had the longest initial run of any show in history.
  There is also a strong tradition of musical theatre in the UK.

- In the 19th century, Gilbert and Sullivan wrote comic operas, often making fun of popular culture and politics. These operas include : HMS Pinafore, The Pirates of Penzance and The Mikado.
  Gilbert and Sullivan's work is still often staged by professional and amateur groups.

- More recently, Andrew Lloyd Webber has written the music for shows which have been popular throughout the world, including in collaboration with Tim Rice :
  Jesus Christ Superstar and Evita, and also Cats and The Phantom of the Opera.

- One British tradition is the pantomime. Many theatres produce a pantomime at Christmas time.
  They are based on fairy stories and are light-hearted plays with music and comedy,
  enjoyed by family audiences. One of the traditional characters is the Dame, a woman played by a man.
  There is often also a pantomime horse or cow played by two actors in the same costume.

- The Edinburgh Festival takes place in Edinburgh, Scotland, every summer.
  It is a series of different arts and cultural festivals, with the biggest and most well-known being the Edinburgh Festival Fringe ('the Fringe'). The Fringe is a showcase of mainly theatre and comedy performances, it often shows experimental work.

- The Laurence Olivier Awards take place annually at different venues in London.
  There are a variety of categories, including : best director, best actor and best actress.
  The awards are named after the British actor Sir Laurence Olivier, later Lord Olivier,
  who was best known for his roles in various Shakespeare plays.

ART

- During the Middle Ages, most art had a religious theme, particularly wall paintings in churches and illustrations in religious books. Much of this was lost after the Protestant Reformation but wealthy families began to collect other paintings and sculptures.

- Many of the painters working in Britain in the 16th and 17th centuries were from abroad - for example : Hans Holbein and Sir Anthony Van Dyck.

- British artists, particularly those painting portraits and landscapes, became well known from the 18th century onwards.

- Works by British and international artists are displayed in galleries across the UK.
  Some of the most well-known galleries are :
  The National Gallery
  Tate Britain and Tate Modern in London
  The National Museum in Cardiff
  The National Gallery of Scotland in Edinburgh.

- The Turner Prize was established in 1984 and celebrates contemporary art.
  It was named after Joseph Turner.
  Four (4) works are shortlisted every year and shown at Tate Britain before the winner is announced.
  The Turner Prize is recognised as one of the most prestigious visual art awards in Europe.
  Previous winners include : Damien Hirst and Richard Wright.

- Tate Modern is based in the former Bankside Power Station in central London.

ARCHITECTURE

- The architectural heritage of the UK is rich and varied.
  In the Middle Ages, great cathedrals and churches were built, many of which still stand today.
  Examples are the cathedrals in : Durham, Lincoln, Canterbury and Salisbury.

- The White Tower in the Tower of London is an example of a Norman castle keep,
  built on the orders of William the Conqueror.

- Gradually, as the countryside became more peaceful and landowners became richer,
  the houses of the wealthy became more elaborate and great country houses such as :
  Hardwick Hall in Derbyshire were built. British styles of architecture began to evolve.

- In the 17th century,
  Inigo Jones took inspiration from classical architecture to design the Queen's House at Greenwich and the
  Banqueting House in Whitehall in London. Later in the century, Sir Christopher Wren helped develop a
  British version of the ornate styles popular in Europe in buildings such as the new St Paul's Cathedral.

- In the 18th century,
  Simpler designs became popular.
  The Scottish architect Robert Adam influenced the development of architecture in the UK, Europe and
  America. He designed the inside decoration as well as the building itself in great houses such as Dumfries
  House in Scotland. His ideas influenced architects in cities such as Bath, where the Royal Crescent was
  built.

- In the 19th century,
  The medieval 'gothic' style became popular again.
  As cities expanded, many great public buildings were built in this style.
  The Houses of Parliament and St Pancras Station were built at this time, as were the town halls in cities
  such as : Manchester and Sheffield.

- In the 20th century,
  Sir Edwin Lutyens had an influence throughout the British Empire.
  He designed New Delhi to be the seat of government in India. After the First World War,
  he was responsible for many war memorials throughout the world, including the Cenotaph in Whitehall.

- The Cenotaph is the site of the annual Remembrance Day service attended by the Queen,
  politicians and foreign ambassadors. The Cenotaph is the centrepiece to the Remembrance Day service,
  unveiled in 1920.

- Modern British architects including : Sir Norman Foster, Lord (Richard) Rogers and Dame Zaha Hadid continue to work on major projects throughout the world as well as within the UK. Alongside the development of architecture, garden design and landscaping have played an important role in the UK.

- In the 18th century,
  Lancelot 'Capability' Brown designed the grounds around country houses so that the landscape appeared to be natural, with grass, trees and lakes. He often said that a place had 'capabilities'. Later, Gertrude Jekyll often worked with Edwin Lutyens to design colourful gardens around the houses he designed.

- Gardens continue to be an important part of homes in the UK.
  The annual Chelsea Flower Show showcases garden design from Britain and around the world.

FASHION AND DESIGN
- Britain has produced many great designers from :
  Thomas Chippendale (who designed furniture in the 18th century) to
  Clarice Cliff (who designed Art Deco ceramics) to
  Sir Terence Conran (a 20th-century interior designer).

- Leading fashion designers of recent years include :
  Mary Quant, Alexander McQueen and Vivienne Westwood.

LITERATURE
- The UK has a prestigious literary history and tradition. Several British writers including :
  the novelist Sir William Golding, the poet Seamus Heaney and the playwright Harold Pinter have won the Nobel Prize in Literature.

- Other authors have become well known in popular fiction. Agatha Christie's detective stories are read all over the world and Ian Fleming's books introduced James Bond.

- In 2003, The Lord of the Rings by JRR Tolkien was voted the country's best-loved novel.

- The Man Booker Prize for Fiction is awarded annually for the best fiction novel written by an author from the : Commonwealth, Ireland or Zimbabwe. It has been awarded since 1968.
  Past winners include : Ian McEwan, Hilary Mantel and Julian Barnes.

BRITISH POETS

- British poetry is among the richest in the world.

- The Anglo-Saxon poem 'Beowulf' tells of its hero's battles against monsters and is still translated into modern English.

- Poems which survive from the Middle Ages include :
  Chaucer's Canterbury Tales' and a poem called Sir Gawain and the Green Knight,
  about one of the knights at the court of King Arthur.

- As well as plays, Shakespeare wrote many sonnets,
  poems which must be fourteen (14) lines long and some longer poems.

- As protestant ideas spread, a number of poets wrote poems inspired by their religious views.
  One of these was John Milton who wrote Paradise Lost.

- Other poets, including William Wordsworth, were inspired by nature,
  Sir Walter Scott wrote poems inspired by Scotland and the traditional stories and songs from the area on the borders of Scotland and England. He also wrote novels, many of which were set in Scotland.

- Poetry was very popular in the 19th century, with poets such as :
  William Blake, John Keats, Lord Byron, Percy Shelley, Alfred Lord Tennyson, and
  Robert and Elizabeth Browning.

- Later, many poets - for example :
  Wilfred Owen and Siegfried Sassoon, were inspired to write about their experiences in the First World War.

- More recently, popular poets have included :
  Sir Walter de la Mare, John Masefield, Sir John Betjeman and Ted Hughes.

- Some of the best-known poets are buried or commemorated in Poet's Corner in Westminster Abbey.
  Some famous lines include :
  Home Thoughts from Abroad by Robert Browning 1812-1889
  She Walks in Beauty by Lord Byron, 1788-1824
  The Daffodils by William Wordsworth, 1770-1850
  The Tyger by William Blake, 1757-1827
  Anthem for Doomed Youth by Wilfred Owen, 1893-1918.

LEISURE

People in the UK spend their leisure time in many different ways.

GARDENING

- A lot of people have gardens at home and will spend their free time looking after them.
  Some people rent additional land called 'an allotment', where they grow fruit and vegetables.
  Gardening and flower shows range from major national exhibitions to small local events.
  Many towns have garden centres selling plants and gardening equipment.

- There are famous gardens to visit throughout the UK, including :
  Kew Gardens
  Sissinghurst and Hidcote in England
  Crathes Castle and Inveraray Castle in Scotland
  Bodnant Garden in Wales
  Mount Stewart in Northern Ireland.

- The countries that make up the UK all have flowers which are particularly associated with them and which
  are sometimes worn on national saints' days :
  England, the rose
  Wales, the daffodil
  Scotland, the thistle
  Northern Ireland, the shamrock.

SHOPPING

- There are many different places to go shopping in the UK.
  Most towns and cities have a central shopping area, which is called the town centre.
  Undercover shopping centres are also common - these might be :
  in town centres or on the outskirts of a town or city.

- Most shops in the UK are open seven (7) days a week,
  although trading hours on Sundays and public holidays are generally reduced.

- Many towns also have markets on one or more days a week, where stallholders sell a variety of goods.

COOKING AND FOOD

- Many people in the UK enjoy cooking. They often invite each other to their homes for dinner.
  A wide variety of food is eaten in the UK because of the country's rich cultural heritage and diverse population.

- There are a variety of foods that are traditionally associated with different parts of the UK.

TRADITIONAL FOODS

- **IN ENGLAND**
  Roast beef, which is served with potatoes, vegetables,
  Yorkshire puddings (batter that is baked in the oven) and other accompaniments.
  Fish and chips are also popular.

- **IN WALES**
  Welsh cakes -
  a traditional Welsh snack made from flour, dried fruits and spices, and served either hot or cold.

- **IN SCOTLAND**
  Haggis - a sheep's stomach stuffed with offal, suet, onions and oatmeal.

- **IN NORTHERN IRELAND**
  Ulster fry -
  a fried meal with bacon, eggs, sausage, black pudding, white pudding, tomatoes, mushrooms, soda bread and potato bread.

FILMS / BRITISH FILM INDUSTRY

- The UK has had a major influence on modern cinema.
  Films were first shown publicly in the UK in 1896 and film screenings very quickly became popular.
  From the beginning, British film makers became famous for clever special effects and this continues to be an area of British expertise. From the early days of the cinema, British actors have worked in both the UK and USA.

- Sir Charles (Charlie) Chaplin became famous in silent movies for his tramp character and was one of many British actors to make a career in Hollywood.

- British studios flourished in the 1930s. Eminent directors included :
  Sir Alexander Korda and Sir Alfred Hitchcock, who later left for Hollywood and remained an important film director until his death in 1980.

- During the Second World War, British movies - for example :
  'In Which We Serve' played an important part in boosting morale. Later, British directors including Sir David Lean and Ridley Scott found great success both in the UK and internationally.

- The 1950s and 1960s were a high point for British comedies, including :
  Passport to Pimlico, The Ladykillers and, later, the 'Carry On' films.

- Many of the films now produced in the UK are made by foreign companies using British expertise.
  Some of the most commercially successful films of all time, including the two (2) highest-grossing film franchises have been produced in the UK : Harry Potter and James Bond.

- Ealing Studios has a claim to being the oldest continuously working film studio facility in the world.
  Britain continues to be particularly strong in special effects and animation, one example is the :
  work of Nick Park, who has won four (4) Oscars for his animated films, including three (3) for films featuring Wallace and Gromit.

- Actors starred in a wide variety of popular films such as :
  Lawrence Olivier, David Niven, Sir Rex Harrison and Richard Burton.
  British actors continue to be popular and continue to win awards throughout the world.
  Recent British actors to have won Oscars include :
  Colin Firth, Sir Anthony Hopkins, Dame Judi Dench, Kate Winslet and Tilda Swinton.

- The annual British Academy Film Awards, hosted by the British Academy of Film and Television Arts (BAFTA), are the British equivalent of the Oscars.

BRITISH COMEDY

- The traditions of comedy and satire, and the ability to laugh at ourselves, are an important part of the UK character.

- Medieval kings and rich nobles had jesters who told jokes and made fun of people in the Court.
Later, Shakespeare included comic characters in his plays.

- In the 18th century, political cartoons attacking prominent politicians - and, sometimes, the monarch or other members of the Royal Family - became increasingly popular.

- In the 19th century, satirical magazines began to be published.
The most famous was Punch, which was published for the first time in the 1840s.

- Today, political cartoons continue to be published in newspapers, and magazines such as :
Private Eye continue the tradition of satire.

- Comedians were a popular feature of British music hall, a form of variety theatre which was very common until television became the leading form of entertainment in the UK.
Some of the people who had performed in the music halls in the 1940s and 1950s, such as :
Morecambe and Wise, became stars of television.

- Television comedy developed its own style.
Situation comedies, or sitcoms, which often look at family life and relationships in the workplace, remain popular. Satire has also continued to be important, with shows like :
'That Was The Week That Was' in the 1960s and 'Spitting Image' in the 1980s and 1990s.

- In 1969, Monty Python's Flying Circus introduced a new type of progressive comedy.
Stand-up comedy, where a solo comedian talks to a live audience, has become popular again in recent years.

TELEVISION AND RADIO

- Many different television (TV) channels are available in the UK.
  Some are free to watch and others require a paid subscription.
  British television shows a wide variety of programmes.
  Popular programmes include regular soap operas such as : Coronation Street and EastEnders.

- In Scotland, some Scotland-specific programmes are shown and there is also a channel with programmes in the Gaelic language. There is a Welsh-language channel in Wales.
  There are also programmes specific to Northern Ireland and some programmes broadcast in Irish Gaelic.

- Everyone in the UK with a TV, computer or other medium which can be used for watching TV
  must have a television licence. One (1) licence covers all of the equipment in one (1) home,
  except when people rent different rooms in a shared house and each has a separate tenancy agreement -
  those people must each buy a separate licence.

- People over seventy-five (75) can apply for a free TV licence and blind people can get a 50% discount.
  You will receive a fine of up to £1,000 if you watch TV but do not have a TV licence.

- The money from TV licences is used to pay for the British Broadcasting Company (BBC).
  This is a British public service broadcaster providing television and radio programmes.
  The BBC is the largest broadcaster in the world.
  It is the only wholly state-funded media organisation that is independent of government.
  Other UK channels are primarily funded through advertisements and subscriptions.

- There are also many different radio stations in the UK.
  Some broadcast nationally and others in certain cities or regions.
  There are radio stations that play certain types of music and some broadcast in regional languages such as : Welsh or Gaelic.

- Like television, BBC radio stations are funded by TV licences and other radio stations are funded through advertisements.

SOCIAL NETWORKING

- Social networking websites such as Facebook and Twitter are a popular way for people to stay in touch with friends, organise social events, and share photos, videos and opinions.
  Many people use social networking on their mobile phones when out and about.

PUBS AND NIGHT CLUBS

- Public houses (pubs) are an important part of the UK social culture.
  Many people enjoy meeting friends in the pub.

- Most communities will have a 'local' pub that is a natural focal point for social activities.
  Pub quizzes are popular. Pool and darts are traditional pub games.

- To buy alcohol in a pub or night club you must be eighteen (18) or over,
  but people under that age may be allowed in some pubs with an adult.
  When they are sixteen (16), people can drink wine or beer with a meal in a hotel or restaurant
  (including eating areas in pubs) as long as they are with someone over eighteen (18).

- Pubs are usually open during the day from 11.00 am (12 noon on Sundays).
  Night clubs with dancing and music usually open and close later than pubs.
  The licensee decides the hours that the pub or night club is open.

BETTING AND GAMBLING

- In the UK, people often enjoy a gamble on sports or other events.
  There are also casinos in many places.

- You have to be eighteen (18) to go into betting shops or gambling clubs.
  There is a National Lottery for which draws are made every week.
  You can enter by buying a ticket or a scratch card.
  People under sixteen (16) are not allowed to participate in the National Lottery.

PETS

- A lot of people in the UK have pets such as cats or dogs.
  They might have them for company or because they enjoy looking after them.
  It is against the law to treat a pet cruelly or to neglect it.

- All dogs in public places must wear a collar showing the name and address of the owner.
  The owner is responsible for keeping the dog under control and for cleaning up after the animal in a public
  place. Vaccinations and medical treatment for animals are available from veterinary surgeons (vets).
  There are charities which may help people who cannot afford to pay a vet.

PLACES OF INTEREST

The UK has a large network of public footpaths in the countryside.
There are also many opportunities for mountain biking, mountaineering and hill walking.
There are fifteen (15) national parks in England, Wales and Scotland.
They are areas of protected countryside that everyone can visit, and where people live,
work and look after the landscape.

- There are many museums in the UK,
  which range from small community museums to large national and civic collections.

- Famous landmarks exist in towns, cities and the countryside throughout the UK.
  Most of them are open to the public to view (generally for a charge).

- Many parts of the countryside and places of interest are kept open by :
  the National Trust in England, Wales and Northern Ireland and the National Trust for Scotland.
  Both are charities that work to : preserve important buildings, coastline and countryside in the UK.

- The National Trust was founded in 1895 by three (3) volunteers.
  There are now more than sixty-one thousand (61,000) volunteers helping to keep the organisation running.

UK LANDMARKS
- Big Ben
- The Eden Project
- Edinburgh Castle
- The Giant's Causeway
- Loch Lomond and the Trossachs National Park
- London Eye
- Snowdonia
- The Tower of London
- The Lake District.

BIG BEN

- Big Ben is the nickname for the great bell of the clock at the Houses of Parliament in London.
  Many people call the clock Big Ben as well.
  The clock is over one hundred and fifty (150) years old and is a popular tourist attraction.
  The clock tower is named 'Elizabeth Tower' in honour of Queen Elizabeth II's Diamond Jubilee in 2012.

THE EDEN PROJECT

- The Eden Project is located in Cornwall, in the south west of England.
  Its biomes, which are like giant greenhouses, house plants from all over the world.
  The Eden Project is also a charity which runs environmental and social projects internationally.

EDINBURGH CASTLE

- The Castle is a dominant feature of the skyline in Edinburgh, Scotland.
  It has a long history, dating back to the early Middle Ages.
  It is looked after by Historic Scotland, a Scottish government agency.

THE GIANT'S CAUSEWAY

- Located on the north-east coast of Northern Ireland,
  the Giant's Causeway is a land formation of columns made from volcanic lava.
  It was formed about fifty (50) million years ago.
  There are many legends about the Causeway and how it was formed.

LOCH LOMOND AND THE TROSSACHS NATIONAL PARK

- This national park covers seven hundred and twenty (720) square miles (1,865 square kilometres)
  in the west of Scotland. Loch Lomond is the largest expanse of fresh water in mainland Britain and
  probably the best-known part of the park.

LONDON EYE

- The London Eye is situated on the southern bank of the River Thames and is a Ferris wheel that is :
  four hundred and forty-three (443) feet (135 metres) tall. It was originally built as part of the UK's
  celebration of the new millennium and continues to be an important part of New Year celebrations.

SNOWDONIA

- Snowdonia is a national park in North Wales.
  It covers an area of eight hundred and thirty-eight (838) square miles (2,170 square kilometres).
  Its most well-known landmark is Snowdon, which is the highest mountain in Wales.

THE TOWER OF LONDON

- The Tower of London was first built by William the Conqueror after he became king in 1066.
  Tours are given by the Yeoman Warders, also known as Beefeaters,
  who tell visitors about the building's history. People can also see the Crown Jewels there.

THE LAKE DISTINCT

- The Lake District is England's largest national park.
  It covers eight hundred and eighty-five (885) square miles (2,292 square kilometres).
  It is famous for its lakes and mountains and is very popular with climbers, walkers and sailors.
  The biggest stretch of water is Windermere.
  In 2007, television viewers voted Wastwater as Britain's favourite view.

THE UK GOVERNMENT

THE DEVELOPMENT OF BRITISH DEMOCRACY
THE BRITISH CONSTITUTION
THE GOVERNMENT
DEVOLVED ADMINISTRATIONS
VISITING PARLIAMENT AND THE DEVOLVED ADMINISTRATIONS
ELECTIONS

CHECK THAT YOU UNDERSTAND

How democracy has developed in the UK
What a constitution is and how the UK's constitution is different from those of most other countries
The role of the monarch
The role of the House of Commons and House of Lords
What the Speaker does
How the UK elects MPs and MEPs
The role of the Prime Minister, cabinet, opposition and shadow cabinet
The role of political parties in the UK system of government
Who the main political parties are
What pressure and lobby groups do
The role of the civil service
The role of local government
The powers of the devolved governments in Wales, Scotland and Northern Ireland
How proceedings in Parliament are recorded
The role of the media in keeping people informed about political issues
Who is eligible to vote
How you register to vote
How to vote
Who can stand for public office
How you can visit Parliament
How you can visit the Welsh Assembly, the Scottish Parliament and the Northern Ireland Assembly

THE DEVELOPMENT OF BRITISH DEMOCRACY

The UK is a parliamentary democracy with the monarch as head of state.
Democracy is a system of government where the whole adult population gets a say.
This might be by direct voting or by choosing representatives to make decisions on their behalf.

- At the turn of the 19th century, Britain was not a democracy as we know it today. Although there were elections to select members of Parliament (MPs), only a small group of people could vote.
  They were men who were : over twenty-one (21) years of age and who owned a certain amount of property.

- The franchise that is, the number of people who had the right to vote grew over the course of the 19th century and political parties began to involve ordinary men and women as members.

- In the 1830s and 1840s, a group called the Chartists campaigned for reform.
  They wanted six (6) changes :
  for every man to have the vote
  elections every year
  for all regions to be equal in the electoral system
  secret ballots
  for any man to be able to stand as an MP
  for MPs to be paid.

- At the time, the campaign was generally seen as a failure.
  However, by 1918 most of these reforms had been adopted.
  The voting franchise was also extended to women over thirty (30), and then in 1928 to men and women over twenty-one (21).

- In 1969, the voting age was reduced to eighteen (18) for men and women.

THE BRITISH CONSTITUTION

A constitution is a set of principles by which a country is governed. It includes all of the institutions that are responsible for running the country and how their power is kept in check.
The constitution also includes laws and conventions.

- The British constitution is not written down in any single document,
  and therefore it is described as : 'unwritten'.
  This is mainly because the UK, unlike America or France, has never had a revolution which led permanently to a totally new system of government.

- Our most important institutions have developed over hundreds of years.

- Some people believe that there should be a single document,
  but others believe an unwritten constitution allows for more flexibility and better government.

CONSTITUTIONAL INSTITUTIONS

- In the UK, there are several different parts of government. The main ones are :
  the monarchy
  the Parliament : the House of Commons and the House of Lords
  the Prime Minister
  the cabinet
  the judiciary (courts)
  the police
  the civil service
  the local government.

- In addition, there are devolved governments in Wales, Scotland and Northern Ireland that have the power to legislate on certain issues.

THE MONARCHY

- Queen Elizabeth II is the head of state of the UK.
  She is also the monarch or head of state of many countries in the Commonwealth.

- The UK has a constitutional monarchy.
  This means that the king or queen does not rule the country but appoints the government,
  which the people have chosen in a democratic election.

- The monarch invites the leader of the party with the largest number of MPs,
  or the leader of a coalition between more than one (1) party, to become the Prime Minister.

- The monarch has regular meetings with the Prime Minister and can : advise, warn and encourage.
  But the decisions on government policies are made by the Prime Minister and cabinet.

- The Queen has reigned since her father's death in 1952, and in 2012 she celebrated her Diamond Jubilee,
  sixty (60) years as queen. She is married to Prince Philip, the Duke of Edinburgh.
  Her eldest son, Prince Charles (the Prince of Wales), is the heir to the throne.

- The Queen has important ceremonial roles, such as the opening of the new parliamentary session each year.
  On this occasion the Queen makes a speech which summarises the government's policies for the year ahead.
  All Acts of Parliament are made in her name.

- The Queen represents the UK to the rest of the world.
  She receives foreign ambassadors and high commissioners,
  entertains visiting heads of state,
  and makes state visits overseas in support of diplomatic and economic relationships with other countries.

- The Queen has an important role in providing stability and continuity.
  While governments and Prime Ministers change regularly, the Queen continues as head of state.
  She provides a focus for national identity and pride, which was demonstrated through the celebrations of
  her jubilee.

SYSTEM OF GOVERNMENT

The system of government in the UK is a parliamentary democracy.
The UK is divided into parliamentary constituencies.
Voters in each constituency elect their member of Parliament (MP) in a General Election.
All of the elected MPs form the House of Commons.
Most MPs belong to a political party, and the party with majority of MPs forms the government.
If one (1) party does not get a majority, two (2) parties can join together to form a coalition.

THE SPEAKER

• Debates in the House of Commons are chaired by the Speaker.
  This person is the chief officer of the House of Commons.
  The speaker is neutral and does not represent a political party, even though he or she is an MP,
  represents a constituency and deals with constituents' problems like any other MP.

• The speaker is chosen by other MPs in a secret ballot.
  The speaker also represents Parliament on ceremonial occasions.
  The speaker keeps order during political debates to make sure the rules are followed.
  This includes making sure the opposition has a guaranteed amount of time to debate issues which it
  chooses.

THE HOUSE OF COMMONS

• The House of Commons is regarded as the more important of the two (2) chambers in Parliament
  because its members are democratically elected.

• The Prime Minister and almost all the members of the cabinet are members of the House of Commons
  (MPs). Each MP represents a parliamentary constituency which is a small area of the country.

• MPs have a number of different responsibilities. They :
  represent everyone in their constituency
  help to create new laws
  scrutinise and comment on what the government is doing
  debate important national issues.

• The House of Commons has powers to overrule the House of Lords, but these are not used often.

THE HOUSE OF LORDS

- Members of the House of Lords, known as peers :
  are not elected by the people and do not represent a constituency.

- The role and membership of the House of Lords has changed over the last fifty (50) years.
  Until 1958, all peers were :
  'hereditary', which means they inherited their title, or
  senior judges, or
  bishops of the Church of England.

- Since 1958, the Prime Minister has had the power to nominate peers just for their own lifetime.
  These are called life peers. They have usually had an important career in :
  politics, business, law or another profession.

- Life peers are appointed by the monarch on the advice of the Prime Minister.
  They also include people nominated :
  by the leaders of the other main political parties or
  by an independent Appointments Commission for non-party peers.

- Since 1999, hereditary peers have lost the automatic right to attend the House of Lords.
  They now elect a few of their number to represent them in the House of Lords.

- The House of Lords is normally more independent of the government than the House of Commons.
  It can suggest amendments or propose new laws, which are then discussed by MPs.

- The House of Lords checks laws that have been passed by the House of Commons to ensure they are fit for purpose. It also holds the government to account to make sure that it is working in the best interests of the people.

- There are peers who are specialists in particular areas, and their knowledge is useful in making and checking laws.

THE GOVERNMENT

THE PRIME MINISTER

- The Prime Minister (PM) is the leader of the political party in power.
  He or she appoints the members of the cabinet and has control over many important public appointments.
  The official home of the Prime Minister is 10 Downing Street, in central London, near the Houses of
  Parliament. He or she also has a country house outside London called Chequers.

- The Prime Minister can be changed if the MPs in the governing party decide to do so, or if he or she wishes
  to resign. The Prime Minister usually resigns if his or her party loses a General Election.

THE CABINET

- The Prime Minister appoints about twenty (20) senior MPs to become ministers in charge of departments.
  These include :
  Chancellor of the Exchequer - responsible for the economy
  Home Secretary - responsible for crime, policing and immigration
  Foreign Secretary - responsible for managing relationships with foreign countries
  Other ministries (called 'Secretaries of State') - responsible for subjects such as :
  education, health and defence.

- These ministers form the cabinet, a committee which usually meets weekly and makes important decisions
  about government policy. Many of these decisions have to be debated or approved by Parliament.
  Each department also has a number of other ministers, called Ministers of State and Parliamentary
  Under-Secretaries of State, who take charge of particular areas of the department's work.

THE OPPOSITION

- The second-largest party in the House of Commons is called the opposition. The leader of the opposition
  usually becomes Prime Minister if his or her party wins the next General Election. The leader of the
  opposition leads his or her party in pointing out what they see as the government's failures and weaknesses.

- One important opportunity to do this is at Prime Minister's Questions, which takes place every week while
  Parliament is sitting. The leader of the opposition also appoints senior opposition MPs to be 'shadow
  ministers'. They form the shadow cabinet and their role is to challenge the government and put forward
  alternative policies.

THE PARTY SYSTEM

- Anyone aged eighteen (18) or over can stand for election as an MP but they are unlikely to win unless they have been nominated to represent one of the major political parties.
These are : the Conservative Party, the Labour Party, the Liberal Democrats, or one (1) of the parties representing Scottish, Welsh or Northern Irish interests.

- There are a few MPs who do not represent any of the main political parties.
They are called 'independents' and usually represent an issue important to their constituency.

- The main political parties actively look for members of the public to join their debates, contribute to their costs, and help at elections for Parliament or for local government.
They have branches in most constituencies and hold policy-making conferences every year.

THE PRESSURE AND LOBBY GROUPS

- Pressure and lobby groups are organisations which try to influence government policy.
They play an important role in politics.
Some are representative organisations such as :
the CBI (Confederation of British Industry), which represents the views of British business.

- Others campaign on particular topics, such as :
the environment, for example : Greenpeace
or human rights, for example : Liberty.

THE CIVIL SERVICE

- Civil servants support the government in developing and implementing its policies.
They also deliver public services.
Civil servants are accountable to ministers.
They are chosen on merit and are politically neutral - they are not political appointees.

- People can apply to join the civil service through an application process, like other jobs in the UK.

- Civil servants are expected to carry out their role with dedication and a commitment to the civil service and its core values. These are : integrity, honesty, objectivity and impartiality (including being politically neutral).

LOCAL GOVERNMENT

- Towns, cities and rural areas in the UK are governed by democratically elected councils, often called 'local authorities'.

- Some areas have both district and county councils, which have different functions. Most large towns and cities have a single local authority.

- Local authorities provide a range of services in their areas. They are funded by money from central government and by local taxes.

- Many local authorities appoint a mayor, who is the ceremonial leader of the council. In some towns, a mayor is elected to be the effective leader of the administration.

- London has thirty-three (33) local authorities, with the Greater London Authority and the Mayor of London coordinating policies across the capital. For most local authorities, local elections for councillors are held in May every year. Many candidates stand for council election as members of a political party.

THE MEDIA AND GOVERNMENT

- Proceedings in Parliament are broadcast on television and published in official reports called Hansard. Written reports can be found in large libraries and at : www.parliament.uk

- Most people get information about political issues and events from : newspapers (often called 'the press') television radio the internet.

- The UK has a free press. This means that what is written in newspapers is free from government control.

- Some newspaper owners and editors hold strong political opinions and run campaigns to try to influence government policy and public opinion.

- By law, radio and television coverage of the political parties must be balanced and so equal time has to be given to rival viewpoints.

DEVOLVED ADMINISTRATIONS

Since 1997, some powers have been devolved from the central government to give people in Wales, Scotland and Northern Ireland more control over matters that directly affect them.

- There has been a Welsh Assembly and a Scottish Parliament since 1999.
  There is also a Northern Ireland Assembly, although this has been suspended on a few occasions.

- Policy and laws governing defence, foreign affairs, immigration, taxation and social security all remain under central UK government control.

- However, many other public services, such as education, are controlled by the devolved administrations. The devolved administrations each have their own civil service.

- Devolved Administrations :
  The Welsh Government and National Assembly for Wales
  The Scottish Parliament
  The Northern Ireland Parliament.

THE WELSH GOVERNMENT

- The Welsh government and National Assembly for Wales are based in Cardiff, the capital city of Wales. The Welsh Assembly Building opened in March 2006.

- The National Assembly has sixty (60) Assembly Members (AMs), and elections are held every four (4) years using a form of proportional representation.
  Members can speak in either Welsh or English, and all of the Assembly's publications are in both languages.

- The Assembly has the power to make laws for Wales in twenty (20) areas, including :
  education and training
  health and social services
  economic development
  housing.

- Since 2011, the National Assembly for Wales has been able to pass laws on these topics without the agreement of the UK Parliament.

THE SCOTTISH PARLIAMENT

- The Scottish Parliament was formed in 1999.
  It sits in Edinburgh, the capital city of Scotland. The Scottish Parliament Building opened in October 2004.

- There are one hundred and twenty-nine (129) Members of the Scottish Parliament (MSPs),
  elected by a form of proportional representation. The Scottish Parliament can pass laws for Scotland on all
  matters which are not specifically reserved to the UK Parliament.
  The matters on which the Scottish Parliament can legislate include :
  civil and criminal law
  health
  education
  planning
  additional tax-raising powers.

THE NORTHERN IRELAND ASSEMBLY

- A Northern Ireland Parliament was established in 1922, when Ireland was divided,
  but it was abolished in 1972, shortly after the Troubles broke out in 1969.
  The Northern Ireland Assembly Building, is known as Stormont.

- The Northern Ireland Assembly was established soon after the Belfast Agreement (or Good Friday
  Agreement) in 1998. There is a power-sharing agreement which distributes ministerial offices amongst the
  main parties.

- The Assembly has one hundred and eight (108) elected members, known as MLAs
  (Members of the Legislative Assembly). They are elected with a form of proportional representation.

- The Northern Ireland Assembly can make decisions on issues such as :
  education
  agriculture
  the environment
  health
  social services.

- The UK Government has the power to suspend all devolved assemblies.
  It has used this power several times in Northern Ireland when local political leaders found it difficult to
  work together. However, the Assembly has been running successfully since 2007.

VISITING PARLIAMENT AND THE DEVOLVED ADMINISTRATIONS

THE UK PARLIAMENT
- The public can listen to debates in the Palace of Westminster from public galleries in both the House of Commons and the House of Lords. You can write to your local MP in advance to ask for tickets or you can queue on the day at the public entrance. Entrance is free. It is usually easier to get in to the House of Lords. Sometimes there are long queues for the House of Commons and people have to wait for at least one (1) or two (2) hours. You can find further information on the UK Parliament at : www.parliament.uk

THE NATIONAL ASSEMBLY FOR WALES
- In Wales the elected members, known as AMs, meet in the Welsh Assembly in the Senedd in Cardiff Bay. The Senedd is an open building. For more information visit : www.wales.gov.uk
  You can book guided tours or seats in the public galleries for the Welsh Assembly.
  To make a booking, contact the :
  Assembly Booking Service
  0845 010 5500
  assembly.bookings@wales.gsi.gov.uk

THE SCOTTISH PARLIAMENT
- In Scotland the elected members, called MSPs, meet in the Scottish Parliament building at Holyrood in Edinburgh. For more information visit : www.scottishparliament.uk
  You can get information, book tickets or arrange tours through visitor services.
  You can write to them at the :
  Scottish Parliament
  Edinburgh, EH99 1SP
  0131 348 5200
  sp.bookings@scottish.parliament.uk

THE NORTHERN IRELAND ASSEMBLY
- In Northern Ireland elected members, known as MLAs, meet in the Northern Ireland Assembly at Stormont, in Belfast. There are two (2) ways to arrange a visit to Stormont. You can either : contact the Education Service, details are on the Northern Ireland Assembly at www.niassembly.gov.uk or contact an MLA.

ELECTIONS

UK ELECTIONS

- MPs are elected at a General Election, which is held at least every five (5) years. If an MP dies or resigns, there will be a fresh election, called a by-election, in his or her constituency. MPs are elected through a system called 'first past the post'. In each constituency, the candidate who gets the most votes is elected. The government is usually formed by the party that wins the majority of constituencies.
If no party wins a majority, two (2) parties may join together to form a coalition.

EUROPEAN PARLIAMENTARY ELECTIONS

- Elections for the European Parliament are also held every five (5) years.
Elected members are called Members of the European Parliament (MEPs).
Elections to the European Parliament use a system of proportional representation, where seats are allocated to each party in proportion to the total number of votes it has won.

CONTACTING ELECTED MEMBERS

- All elected member have a duty to serve and represent their constituents. You can get contact details for all your representatives and their parties from your local library and from : www.parliament.uk

- These are also listed in The Phone Book, published by BT, and in Yellow Pages :
Members of the Parliament (MPs)
Assembly Members (AMs)
Members of the Scottish Parliament (MSPs)
Members of the European Parliament (MEPs).

- You can contact MPs by letter or telephone at their constituency office, or at their office in the House of Commons.
The House of Commons
Westminster, London
SW1A 0AA
020 7729 3000

- In addition, many MPs, AMs, MSPs and MEPs hold regular 'surgeries', where constituents can go in person to talk about issues that are of concern to them. These surgeries are often advertised in the local newspaper.

WHO CAN VOTE?

- The UK has had a fully democratic voting system since 1928.

- The present voting age of eighteen (18) was set in 1969 and (with a few exceptions) all UK-born and naturalised adult citizens have the right to vote.

- Adult citizens of the UK, and citizens of the Commonwealth and the Irish Republic who are resident in the UK, can vote in all public elections. Adult citizens of other EU States who are resident in the UK can vote in all elections except General Elections.

WHERE TO VOTE?

- People vote in elections at places called polling stations, or polling places in Scotland.
  Before the election you will be sent a poll card.
  This tells you : where your polling station or polling place is and when the election will take place.

- On election day, the polling station or place will be open from : 7.00 am until 10.00 pm.
  When you arrive at the polling station, the staff will ask for your name and address.
  In Northern Ireland you will also have to show photographic identification.
  You will then get your ballot paper, which you take to a polling booth to fill in privately.
  You should make up your own mind who to vote for.
  No one has the right to make you vote for a particular candidate.
  You should follow the instructions on the ballot paper.
  Once you have completed it, put it in the ballot box.

- If it is difficult for you to get to a polling station or polling place,
  you can register for a postal ballot.
  Your ballot paper will be sent to your home before the election.
  You then fill it in and post it back.
  You can choose to do this when you register to vote.

THE ELECTORAL REGISTER

- To be able to vote in a parliamentary, local or European elections,
  you must have your name on the electoral register.

- If you are eligible to vote, you can register by contacting your local council electoral registration office.
  This is usually based at your local council (in Scotland it may be based elsewhere).
  If you don't know which local authority you come under, you can find out by visiting :
  www.aboutmyvote.co.uk and entering your post code.

- You can also download voter registration forms in English, Welsh and some other languages.

- The electoral register is updated every year in September or October.
  An electoral registration form is sent to every household and this has to be completed and returned
  with the names of everyone who is resident in the household and eligible to vote.

- In Northern Ireland a different system operates. This is called 'individual registration' and all those entitled
  to vote must complete their own registration form. Once registered, people stay on the register provided
  their personal details do not change. For more information see the Electoral Office for Northern Ireland at :
  www.eoni.org.uk

- By law, each local authority has to make its electoral register available for anyone to look at,
  although this has to be supervised.
  The register is kept at each local electoral registration office (or council office in England and Wales).
  It is also possible to see the register at some public buildings such as libraries.

STANDING FOR OFFICE

- Most citizens of the UK, the Irish Republic or the Commonwealth aged eighteen (18) or over can stand
  for public office. There are some exceptions, including :
  members of the armed forces
  civil servants
  people found guilty of certain criminal offences

- Members of the House of Lords may not stand for election to the House of Commons but are eligible for all
  other public offices.

THE LAW AND YOUR ROLE

RESPECTING THE LAW
THE ROLE OF THE COURTS
FUNDAMENTAL PRINCIPLES
TAXATION
DRIVING
YOUR ROLE IN THE COMMUNITY
HOW YOU CAN SUPPORT YOUR COMMUNITY
LOOKING AFTER THE ENVIRONMENT

CHECK THAT YOU UNDERSTAND

The difference between civil and criminal law and some examples of each
The duties of the police
The possible terrorist threats facing the UK
The role of the judiciary
About the different criminal courts in the UK
About the different civil courts in the UK
How you can settle a small claim
The fundamental principles of UK Law
That domestic violence, FGM and forced marriage are illegal in the UK
The system of income tax and National Insurance
The requirements for driving a car
The different ways you can help at your child's school
The role of school governors and members of school boards, and how you can become one
The role of members of political parties
The different local services people can volunteer to support
How to donate blood and organs
The benefits of volunteering for you, other people and the community
The types of activities that volunteers can do
How you can look after the environment

RESPECTING THE LAW

One of the most important responsibilities of all residents in the UK is to **'know and obey the law'**. Britain is proud of being a welcoming country, but all residents, regardless of their background, are expected to comply with the law and to understand that some things which may be allowed in other legal systems are not acceptable in the UK. Those who do not respect the law should not expect to be allowed to become permanent residents in the UK. The law is relevant to all areas of life in the UK. You should make sure that you are aware of the laws which affect your everyday life, including both your personal and business affairs.

THE LAW IN THE UK

- Every person in the UK receives equal treatment under the law.
  This means that the law applies in the same way to everyone, no matter who they are or where they are from. Laws can be divided into : criminal law and civil law.

- **CRIMINAL LAW** - relates to crimes, which are usually investigated by the police or another authority such as a council, and which are punished by the courts.
  Examples of criminal laws are :
  Carrying a weapon
  Drugs
  Racial crime
  Selling tobacco
  Smoking in public places
  Buying alcohol
  Drinking in public.

  This list does not include all crimes.
  There are many that apply in most countries, such as : murder, theft and assault.
  You can find out more about types of crime in the UK at : www.gov.uk

- **CIVIL LAW** - is used to settle disputes between individuals or groups.
  Examples of civil laws are :
  Housing law
  Consumers rights
  Employment law
  Debt.

CARRYING A WEAPON
It is a criminal offence to carry a weapon of any kind, even if it is for self-defence.
This includes a gun, a knife or anything that is made or adapted to cause injury.

DRUGS
Selling or buying drugs such as : heroin, cocaine, ecstasy and cannabis is illegal in the UK.

RACIAL CRIME
It is a criminal offence to cause harassment, alarm or distress to someone because of their religion or ethnic origin.

SELLING TOBACCO
It is illegal to sell tobacco products to anyone under the age of eighteen (18) -
for example : cigarettes, cigars, roll-up tobacco.

SMOKING IN PUBLIC PLACES
It is against the law to smoke tobacco products in nearly every enclosed public place in the UK.
There are signs displayed to tell you where you cannot smoke.

BUYING ALCOHOL
It is a criminal offence to sell alcohol to anyone who is under eighteen (18) or to buy alcohol for people who are under the age of eighteen (18). There is one exception : people aged sixteen (16) or over can drink alcohol with a meal in a hotel or restaurant.

DRINKING IN PUBLIC
Some places have alcohol-free zones where you cannot drink in public. The police can also confiscate alcohol or move young people on from public places. You can be fined or arrested.

HOUSING LAW
This includes disputes between landlords and tenants over issues such as : repairs and eviction.

CONSUMER RIGHTS
An example of this is a dispute about faulty goods or services.

EMPLOYMENT LAW
These cases include disputes over wages and cases of unfair dismissal or discrimination in the workplace.

DEBT
People might be taken to court if they owe money to someone.

THE POLICE AND THEIR DUTIES

- The police are organised into a number of separate police forces headed by Chief Constables. They are independent of the government.

- The job of the police in the UK is to :
  protect life and property
  prevent disturbances (also known as keeping the peace)
  prevent and detect crime.

- In November 2012, the public elected Police and Crime Commissioners (PCCs) in England and Wales. These are directly elected individuals who are responsible for the delivery of an efficient and effective police force that reflects the needs of their local communities.

- PCCs set local police priorities and the local policing budget. They also appoint the local Chief Constable. The police force is a public service that helps and protects everyone, no matter what their background or where they live.

- Police officers must themselves obey the law.
  They must not : misuse their authority, make a false statement, be rude or abusive, or commit racial discrimination. If police officers are corrupt or misuse their authority they are severely punished.

- Police officers are supported by police community support officers (PCSOs).
  PCSOs have different roles according to the area but usually :
  patrol the streets, work with the public and support police officers at crime scenes and major events.

- All people in the UK are expected to help the police prevent and detect crimes whenever they can. If you are arrested and taken to a police station, a police officer will tell you the reason for your arrest and you will be able to seek legal advice.

- If something goes wrong, the police complaints system tries to put it right.
  Anyone can make a complaint about the police by :
  going to a police station or writing to the Chief Constable of the police force involved.

- Complaints can also be made to an independent body :
  the Independent Police Complaints Commissioner in England and Wales
  the Police Complaints Commissioner for Scotland or
  the Police Ombudsman for Northern Ireland.

TERRORISM AND EXTREMISM

- The UK faces a range of terrorist threats.
  The most serious of these is from Al Qa'ida, its affiliates and like-minded organisations.
  The UK also faces threats from other kinds of terrorism, such as Northern Ireland-related terrorism.

- All terrorist groups try to radicalise and recruit people to their cause.
  How, where and to what extent they try to do so will vary.
  Evidence shows that these groups attract very low levels of public support,
  but people who want to make their home in the UK should be aware of this threat.

- It is important that all citizens feel safe. This includes feeling safe from all kinds of extremism (vocal or active opposition to fundamental British values), including religious extremism and far-right extremism.

- If you think someone is trying to persuade you to join an extremist or terrorist cause, you should notify your local police force.

THE ROLE OF THE COURTS

THE JUDICIARY

- Judges (who are together called 'the judiciary') are responsible for interpreting the law and ensuring that trials are conducted fairly. The government cannot interfere with this.

- Sometimes the actions of the government are claimed to be illegal.
  If the judges agree, then the government must either change its policies or ask Parliament to change the law.
  If the judges find that a public body is not respecting someone's legal rights, they can order that body to change its practices and / or pay compensation.

- Judges also make decisions in disputes between members of the public or organisations.
  These might be about contracts, property or employment rights or after an accident.

- The 'Old Bailey' is probably the most famous criminal court in the world.

- There are some differences between the court systems in :
  England and Wales, Scotland and Northern Ireland.

- **CRIMINAL COURTS**
  Magistrates' and Justice of the Peace Courts
  Crown Courts and Sheriff Court
  Youth Courts

- **CIVIL COURTS**
  County Courts
  The Small Claims Procedure

MAGISTRATES' AND JUSTICE OF THE PEACE COURTS

- In England, Wales and Northern Ireland, most minor criminal cases are dealt with in a Magistrates' Court. In Scotland, minor criminal offences go to a Justice of the Peace Court.

- Magistrates and Justices of the Peace (JPs) are members of the local community.
  In England, Wales and Scotland, they usually work unpaid and do not need legal qualifications.
  They receive training to do the job and are supported by a legal adviser.
  Magistrates decide the verdict in each case that comes before them and,
  if the person is found guilty, the sentence that they are given. In Northern Ireland,
  cases are heard by a District Judge or Deputy District Judge, who is legally qualified and paid.

CROWN COURTS AND SHERIFF COURTS

- In England, Wales and Northern Ireland, serious offences are tried in front of a judge and a jury in a Crown Court. In Scotland, serious cases are heard in a Sheriff Court with either a sheriff or a sheriff with a jury. The most serious cases in Scotland such as murder, are heard at a High Court with a judge and jury.

- A jury is made up of members of the public chosen at random from the local electoral register.
  In England, Wales and Northern Ireland, a jury has twelve (12) members.
  In Scotland, a jury has fifteen (15) members.

- Everyone who is summoned to do jury service must do it unless they are not eligible - for example :
  because they have a criminal conviction or they provide a good reason to be excused, such as ill health.
  The jury has to listen to the evidence presented at the trial and then decide a verdict of 'guilty' or
  'not guilty' based on what they have heard. In Scotland, a third (3rd) verdict of 'not proven' is also possible.
  If the jury finds a defendant guilty, the judge decides on the penalty.

YOUTH COURTS

- In England, Wales and Northern Ireland, if an accused person is aged ten (10) to seventeen (17) years old the case is normally heard in a Youth Court in front of up to three (3) specially trained magistrates or a District Judge. The most serious cases will go to the Crown Court. The parents or carers of the young person are expected to attend the hearing. Members of the public are not allowed in Youth Courts, and the name or photographs of the accused young person cannot be published in newspaper, or used by the media.

- In Scotland a system called the Children's Hearings System is used to deal with children and young people who have committed an offence. Northern Ireland has a system of youth conferencing to consider how a child should be dealt with when they have committed an offence.

COUNTY COURTS

- County Courts deal with a wide range of civil disputes. These include people trying to : get back money that is owed to them, cases involving personal injury, family matters, breaches of contract and divorce. In Scotland, most of these matters are dealt with in the Sheriff Court. More serious civil cases - for example : when a large amount of compensation is being claimed - are dealt with in the High Court in England, Wales and Northern Ireland. In Scotland, they are dealt with in the Court of Session in Edinburgh.

THE SMALL CLAIMS PROCEDURE

- The small claims procedure is an informal way of helping people to settle minor disputes without spending a lot of time and money using a lawyer. This procedure is used for claims of :
  in England and Wales   less than £5,000
  in Scotland and Northern Ireland   less than £3,000

- The hearing is held in front of a judge in an ordinary room, and people from both sides of the dispute sit around a table. Small claims can also be issued online through :
  Money Claims Online - www.moneyclaim.gov.uk

- You can get details about the small claims procedure from your local County Court or Sheriff Court. Details of your local court can be found as follows :
  in England and Wales   www.gov.uk
  in Scotland   www.scotcourts.gov.uk
  in Northern Ireland   www.courtsni.gov.uk

LEGAL ADVICE

- Solicitors are trained lawyers who : give advice on legal matters, take action for their clients and represent their clients in court. There are solicitors' offices throughout the UK. It is important to find out which aspects of law a solicitor specialises in and to check that they have the right experience to help you with your case. Many advertise in local newspapers and in Yellow Pages. Solicitors' charges are usually based on how much time they spend on a case. It is very important to find out at the start how much a case is likely to cost. The Citizens Advice Bureau can give you names of local solicitors and which areas of law they specialise in : www.citizensadvice.org.uk

- You can also get this information from :
  the Law Society in England and Wales   www.lawsociety.org.uk
  the Law Society of Scotland   www.lawscot.org.uk
  the Law Society of Northern Ireland   www.lawsoc-ni.org

FUNDAMENTAL PRINCIPLES

Britain has a long history of respecting an individual's rights and ensuring essential freedoms.
These rights have their roots in Magna Carta. The Habeas Corpus Act and the Bill of Rights of 1689,
and they have developed over a period of time. British diplomats and lawyers had an important role in
drafting the European Convention on Human Rights and Fundamental Freedoms.
The UK was one of the first countries to sign the Convention in 1950.

- The Human Rights Act 1998 incorporated the European Convention on Human Rights into UK Law.
  The government, public bodies and the courts must follow the principles of the Convention.
  Some of the principles included in the European Convention on Human Rights are :
  right to life
  prohibition of torture
  prohibition of slavery and forced labour
  right to liberty and security
  right to a fair trial
  freedom of thought, conscience and religion
  freedom of expression (speech).

EQUAL OPPORTUNITIES

- UK Laws ensure that people are not treated unfairly in any area of life or work because of their :
  age, disability, sex, pregnancy and maternity, race, religion or belief, sexuality or marital status.
  If you face problems with discrimination, you can get more information from -
  the Citizens Advice Bureau or from one of the following organisations :

- In England and Wales,
  Equality and Human Rights Commission
  www.equalityhumanrights.com

- In Scotland,
  Equality and Human Rights Commission in Scotland and Scottish Human Rights Commission
  www.equalityhumanrights.com/scotland/the-commission-in-scotland
  www.scottishhumanrights.com

- In Northern Ireland,
  Equality Commission for Northern Ireland and Northern Ireland Human Rights Commission
  www.equalityni.org and www.nihrc.org

DOMESTIC VIOLENCE

- In the UK, brutality and violence in the home is a serious crime. Anyone who is violent towards their partner - can be prosecuted - whether they are : a man or a woman, married or living together.
Any man who forces a woman to have sex, including a woman's husband, can be charged with rape.

- It is important for anyone facing domestic violence to get help as soon as possible.
A solicitor or the Citizens Advice Bureau can explain the available options.

- In some areas there are safe places to go and stay in, called refuges or shelters.
There are emergency telephone numbers in the helpline section at the front of Yellow Pages, including, for women, the number of the nearest women's centre.

- You can also phone the twenty-four (24)-hour National Domestic Violence Freephone Helpline at any time, or the police can help you find a safe place to stay.
National Domestic Violence Freephone Helpline
0808 2000 247

FEMALE GENITAL MUTILATION

- Female genital mutilation (FGM), also known as cutting or female circumcision, is illegal in the UK.
Practising FGM or taking a girl or woman abroad for FGM is a criminal offence.

FORCED MARRIAGE

- A marriage should be entered into with the full and free consent of both people involved.
Arranged marriages, where both parties agree to the marriage, are acceptable in the UK.
Forced marriage is where one or both parties do not or cannot give their consent to enter into the partnership. Forcing another person to marry is a criminal offence.

- Forced Marriage Protection Orders were introduced in 2008 for
England, Wales and Northern Ireland under the Forced Marriage (Civil Protection) Act 2007.
Court orders can be obtained to protect a person from being forced into a marriage, or to protect a person in a forced marriage. Similar Protection Orders were introduced in Scotland in November 2011.

- A potential victim, or someone acting for them, can apply for an order.
Anyone found to have breached an order can be jailed for up to two (2) years for contempt of court.

TAXATION

INCOME TAX

- People in the UK have to pay tax on their income, which includes :
  wages from paid employment
  profits from self-employment
  taxable benefits
  pensions
  income from property
  savings and dividends.

- Money raised from income tax pays for government services such as :
  roads
  education
  police
  the armed forces.

- For most people, the right amount of income tax is automatically taken from their income from employment by their employer and paid directly to HM Revenue & Customs (HMRC), the government department that collects taxes. This system is called 'Pay As You Earn' (PAYE).

- If you are self-employed, you need to pay your own tax through a system called 'self-assessment', which includes completing a tax return.

- Other people may also need to complete a tax return.
  If HMRC sends you a tax return, it is important to complete and return the form as soon as you have all the necessary information.

- You can find out more about income tax at : www.hmrc.gov.uk/incometax

- You can get help and advice about taxes and completing tax forms from the HMRC self-assessment helpline and website :
  HMRC Self-Assessment Helpline
  0845 300 0627
  www.hmrc.gov.uk

NATIONAL INSURANCE

- Almost everybody in the UK who is in paid work, including self-employed people, must pay National Insurance Contributions.

- The money raised from National Insurance Contributions is used to pay for state benefits and services such as : the state retirement pension and the National Health Service (NHS).

- Employees have their National Insurance Contributions deducted from their pay by their employer. People who are self-employed need to pay National Insurance Contributions themselves.

- Anyone who does not pay enough National Insurance Contributions will not be able to receive certain contributory benefits such as : Jobseeker's Allowance or a full state retirement pension.
Some workers, such as part-time workers, may not qualify for statutory payments such as maternity pay if they do not earn enough.

- Further guidance about National Insurance Contributions is available on HMRC's website at : www.hmrc.gov.uk/ni

GETTING A NATIONAL INSURANCE NUMBER

- A National Insurance number is a unique personal account number. It makes sure that the National Insurance Contributions and tax you pay are properly recorded against your name. All young people in the UK are sent a National Insurance number just before their sixteenth (16th) birthday.

- A non-UK national living in the UK and looking for work, starting work or setting up as self-employed will need a National Insurance number. However, you can start work without one.

- If you have permission to work in the UK, you will need to telephone the Department for Work and Pensions (DWP) to arrange to get a National Insurance number. You may be required to attend an interview.

- The DWP will advise you of the appropriate application process and tell you which documents you will need to bring to an interview if one is necessary. You will usually need documents to prove your identity and that you have permission to work in the UK. A National Insurance number does not on its own prove to an employer that you have the right to work in the UK.

- You can find out more information about how to apply for a National Insurance number at : www.gov.uk

DRIVING

- In the UK, you must be at least seventeen (17) years old to drive a car or motor cycle and you must have a driving licence to drive on public roads.

- To get a UK driving licence, you must pass a driving test, which tests both : your knowledge and your practical skills.

- You need to be at least sixteen (16) years old to ride a moped, and there are other age requirements and special tests for driving large vehicles.

- Drivers can use their driving licence until they are seventy (70) years old. After that, the licence is valid for three (3) years at a time.

- In Northern Ireland, a newly qualified driver must display an 'R' plate (for restricted driver) for one (1) year after passing the test.

- If your driving licence is from a country in the European Union (EU), Iceland, Liechtenstein or Norway, you can drive in the UK for as long as your licence is valid.

- If you have a licence from any other country, you may use it in the UK for up to twelve (12) months. To continue driving after that, you must get a UK full driving licence.

- If you are a resident in the UK, your car or motor cycle must be registered at the Driver and Vehicle Licensing Agency (DVLA). You must pay an annual vehicle tax and display the tax disc, which shows that the tax has been paid, on the windscreen. You must also have valid motor insurance. It is a serious criminal offence to drive without insurance.

- If your vehicle is over three (3) years old, you must take it for a Ministry of Transport (MOT) test every year. It is an offence not to have an MOT certificate if your vehicle is more than three (3) years old.

- You can find out more about vehicle tax and MOT requirements from : www.gov.uk

YOUR ROLE IN THE COMMUNITY

Becoming a British citizen or settling in the UK brings responsibilities but also opportunities. Everyone has the opportunity to participate in their community.

VALUES AND RESPONSIBILITIES
- Although Britain is one of the world's most diverse societies, there is a set of shared values and responsibilities that everyone can agree with. Taking on these values and responsibilities will make it easier for you to become a full and active citizen. These values and responsibilities include :
  to obey and respect the law
  to be aware of the rights of others and respect those rights
  to treat others with fairness
  to behave responsibly
  to help and protect your family
  to respect and preserve the environment
  to treat everyone equally, regardless of : sex, race, religion, age, disability, class or sexual orientation
  to work to provide for yourself and your family
  to help others
  to vote in local and national government elections.

BEING A GOOD NEIGHBOUR
- When you move into a new house or apartment, introduce yourself to the people who live near you. Getting to know your neighbours can help you to become part of the community and make friends. Your neighbours are also a good source of help - for example :
  they may be willing to feed your pets if you are away, or offer advice on local shops and services. You can help prevent any problems and conflicts with your neighbours by respecting their privacy and limiting how much noise you make. Also try to keep your garden tidy, and only put your refuse bags and bins on the street or in communal areas if they are due to be collected.

GETTING INVOLVED IN LOCAL ACTIVITIES
- Volunteering and helping your community are an important part of being a good citizen. They enable you to integrate and get to know other people.
  It helps to make your community a better place if residents support each other.
  It also helps you to fulfil your duties as a citizen, such as : behaving responsibly and helping others.

122

HOW YOU CAN SUPPORT YOUR COMMUNITY

There are a number of positive ways in which you can support your community and be a good citizen.

JURY SERVICE
- As well as getting the right to vote, people on the electoral register are randomly selected to serve on a jury. Anyone who is on the electoral register and is aged eighteen (18) to seventy (70) can be asked to do this.

HELPING IN SCHOOLS
- If you have children, there are many ways in which you can help at their schools.
  Parents can often help in classrooms, by supporting activities or listening to children read.
  Many schools organise events to raise money for extra equipment or out-of-school activities.
  Activities might include : book sales, toy sales or bringing food to sell.

- You might have good ideas of your own for raising money. Sometimes events are organised by Parent-Teacher Associations (PTAs). Volunteering to help with their events or joining the association is a way of doing something good for the school and also making new friends in your local community.
  You can find out about these opportunities from notices in the school or notes your children bring home.

SCHOOL GOVERNORS AND SCHOOL BOARDS
- School governors, or members of the school board in Scotland, are people from the local community who wish to make a positive contribution to children's education. They must be aged eighteen (18) or over at the date of their election or appointment. There is no upper age limit.
  Governors and school boards have an important part to play in raising school standards.

- They have three (3) key roles :
  setting the strategic direction of the school
  ensuring accountability
  monitoring and evaluating school performance.

- You can contact your local school to ask if they need a new governor or school board member.
  In England, you can also apply online at the School Governors' One-Stop Shop at : www.sgoss.org.uk
  In England, parents and other community groups can apply to open a free school in their local area.
  More information about this can be found on the Department for Education at : www.dfe.gov.uk

SUPPORTING POLITICAL PARTIES

- Political parties welcome new members. Joining one is a way to demonstrate your support for certain views and to get involved in the democratic process. Political parties are particularly busy at election times. Members work hard to persuade people to vote for their candidates - for instance :
by handing out leaflets in the street or by knocking on people's doors and asking for their support.
This is called 'canvassing'. You don't have to tell a canvasser how you intend to vote if you don't want to.
British citizens can stand for office as : a local councillor, a member of Parliament
(or the devolved equivalents) or a member of the European Parliament.
This is an opportunity to become even more involved in the political life of the UK.

- You may also be able to stand for office if you are : an Irish citizen, an eligible Commonwealth citizen or (except for standing to be an MP) a citizen of another EU country.
You can find out more about joining a political party from the individual party websites.

HELPING WITH LOCAL SERVICES

- There are opportunities to volunteer with a wide range of local service providers,
including local hospitals and youth projects. Services often want to involve local people in decisions about the way in which they work. Universities, housing associations, museums and arts councils may advertise for people to serve as volunteers in their governing bodies. You can volunteer with the police, and become a special constable or a lay (non-police) representative. You can also apply to become a magistrate.
You will often find advertisements for vacancies in your local newspaper or on local radio.
You can also find out more about these sorts of roles at : www.gov.uk

BLOOD AND ORGAN DONATION

- Donated blood is used by hospitals to help people with a wide range of injuries and illnesses.
Giving blood only takes about an hour to do. You can register to give blood :

in England	www.blood.co.uk
in North Wales	www.blood.co.uk
rest of Wales	www.welsh-blood.org.uk
in Scotland	www.scotblood.co.uk
in Northern Ireland	www.nibts.org

- Many people in the UK are waiting for organ transplants.
If you register to be an organ donor, it can make it easier for your family to decide whether to donate your organs when you die. Living people can also donate a kidney.
You can register to be an organ donor at : www.organdonation.nhs.uk

OTHER WAYS TO VOLUNTEER

- Volunteering is working for good causes without payment. There are many benefits to volunteering, such as : meeting new people and helping make your community a better place. Some volunteer activities will give you : a chance to practise your English, or develop work skills that will help you find a job, or improve your Curriculum Vitae (CV). Many people volunteer simply because they want to help other people.
Activities you can do as a volunteer include :
working with animals - for example : **caring for animals at a local rescue shelter**
youth work - for example : **volunteering at a youth group**
helping improve the environment - for example : **participating in a litter pick-up in the local area**
working with the homeless in - for example : **a homelessness shelter**
mentoring - for example : **supporting someone who has just come out of prison**
work in health and hospitals - for example : **working on an information desk in a hospital**
helping older people at - for example : **a residential care home.**

- There are thousands of active charities and voluntary organisations in the UK.
They work to improve the lives of people, animals and the environment in many different ways.
They range from the British branches of international organisations, such as the British Red Cross,
to small local charities working in particular areas, they include charities working :
with older people, such as : **Age UK**
with the homeless, - for example : **Crisis and Shelter**
with children, - for example : **National Society for the Prevention of Cruelty to Children (NSPCC)**
there are also medical research charities, - for example : **Cancer Research UK**
environmental charities, including the : **National Trust and Friends of the Earth**
charities working with animal charities, such as : the **People's Dispensary for Sick Animals (PDSAI).**

- Volunteers are needed to help with their activities and to raise money. The charities often advertise in local newspapers, and most have websites that include information about their opportunities.
You can also get information about volunteering for different organisations from : www.do-it.org.uk

- There are many opportunities for younger people to volunteer and receive accreditation which will help them to develop their skills. These include the National Citizen Service programme, which gives sixteen (16) and seventeen (17) year-olds the opportunity to : enjoy outdoor activities, develop their skills and take part in a community project. You can find out more about these opportunities as follows :

National Citizen Service	www.nationalcitizenservice.direct.gov.uk
in England	www.vinspired.com
in Wales	www.gwirvol.org
in Scotland	www.vds.org.uk
in Northern Ireland	www.volunteernow.co.uk

LOOKING AFTER THE ENVIRONMENT

It is important to recycle as much of your waste as you can. Using recycled materials to make
new products uses less energy and means that we do not need to extract more raw materials from the earth.
It also means that less rubbish is created, so the amount being put into landfill is reduced.

- You can learn more about recycling and its benefits at : www.recyclenow.com
  At this website you can also find out what you can recycle at home and in the local area if you live in
  England. This information is available :
  for Wales   www.wasteawarenesswales.org.uk
  for Scotland   www.recycleforscotland.com
  for Northern Ireland   from your local authority.

- A good way to support your local community is to shop for products locally where you can.
  This will help businesses and farmers in your area and in Britain.
  It will also reduce your carbon footprint, because the products you buy will not have had to travel as far.

- Walking and using public transport to get around when you can is also a good way to
  protect the environment. It means that you create less pollution than when you use a car.

NOTABLE BRITISH PEOPLE AND THEIR WORKS

THE SIX (6) WIVES OF HENRY VIII
WILLIAM SHAKESPEARE
ISAAC NEWTON
ROBERT BURNS
RICHARD ARKWRIGHT
SAKE DEAN MAHOMET
ISAMBARD KINGDOM BRUNEL
FLORENCE NIGHTINGALE
EMMELINE PANKHURST
RUDYARD KIPLING
WINSTON CHURCHILL
ALEXANDER FLEMING
CLEMENT ATTLEE
WILLIAM BEVERIDGE
RICHARD AUSTEN BUTLER
DYLAN THOMAS
MARY PETERS
MARGARET THATCHER
ROALD DAHL
SOME GREAT BRITISH INVENTIONS OF THE 20TH CENTURY
NOTABLE BRITISH SPORTSMEN AND WOMEN
NOTABLE COMPOSERS
MORE RECENT, IMPORTANT COMPOSERS
NOTABLE BRITISH ARTISTS
NOTABLE AUTHORS AND WRITERS
SOME FAMOUS LINES
SOME FAMOUS BRITISH FILMS

CHECK THAT YOU UNDERSTAND
British people and their contributions
British Inventions of the 20th Century (you do not need to remember dates of births and deaths)
Important figures in British literature

THE SIX (6) WIVES OF HENRY VIII

CATHERINE OF ARAGON
Catherine was a Spanish princess.
She and Henry had a number of children but only one, Mary, survived.
When Catherine was too old to give him another child, Henry decided to divorce her, hoping that another wife would give him a son to be his heir.

ANNE BOLEYN
Anne Boleyn was English. She and Henry had one daughter, Elizabeth.
Anne was unpopular in the country and was accused of taking lovers.
She was executed at the Tower of London.

JANE SEYMOUR
Henry married Jane after Anne's execution.
She gave Henry the son he wanted, Edward, but she died shortly after the birth.

ANNE OF CLEVES
Anne was a German princess.
Henry married her for political reasons but divorced her soon after.

CATHERINE HOWARD
Catherine was a cousin of Anne Boleyn.
She was also accused of taking lovers and executed.

CATHERINE PARR
Catherine was a widow who married Henry late in his life,
She survived him and married again but died soon after.

WILLIAM SHAKESPEARE
(1564-1616)
- Shakespeare was born in Stratford-upon-Avon, England.
  He was a playwright and actor and wrote many poems and plays.
  His most famous plays include : A Midsummer Night's Dream, Hamlet, Macbeth, Romeo and Juliet.

- He also dramatised significant events from the past, but he did not focus solely on kings and queens.
  He was one of the first to portray ordinary Englishmen and women.
  Shakespeare had a great influence on the English language and invented many words that are still common
  today. Lines from his plays and poems which are often still quoted include :
  'once more unto the breach'   from Henry V
  'to be or not to be'   from Hamlet
  'a rose by any other name'   from Romeo and Juliet
  'all the world's a stage'   from As You Like It
  'the darling buds of May'   from Sonnet 18 - Shall I Compare Thee to A Summer's Day.

- Many people regard Shakespeare as the greatest playwright of all time.
  His plays and poems are still performed and studied in Britain and other countries today.
  The Globe Theatre in London is a modern copy of the theatres in which his plays were first performed.

ISAAC NEWTON
(1643-1727)
- Born in Lincolnshire, eastern England. Isaac Newton first became interested in science when he studied at
  Cambridge University. He became an important figure in the field. His most famous published work was
  Philosophiae Naturalis Principia Mathematica ('Mathematical Principles of Natural Philosophy'),
  which showed how gravity applied to the whole universe. Newton also discovered that white light is made
  up of the colours of the rainbow. Many of his discoveries are still important for modern science.

ROBERT BURNS
(1759-1796)
- Known in Scotland as 'The Bard', Robert Burns was a Scottish poet.
  He wrote in the Scots language, English with some Scottish words, and standard English.
  He also revised a lot of traditional folk songs by changing or adding lyrics. Burns' best-known work is
  probably the song Auld Lang Syne, which is sung by people in the UK and other countries when they are
  celebrating the New Year (or Hogmanay as it is called in Scotland).

RICHARD ARKWRIGHT
(1732-1792)
- Born in 1732, Arkwright originally trained and worked as a barber. He was able to dye hair and make wigs.
When wigs became less popular, he started to work in textiles. He improved the original carding machine.
Carding is the process of preparing fibres for spinning into yarn and fabric.
He also developed horse-driven spinning mills that used only one machine.
This increased the efficiency of production. Later, he used the steam engine to power machinery.
Arkwright is particularly remembered for the efficient and profitable way that he ran his factories.

SAKE DEAN MAHOMET
(1759-1851)
- Mahomet was born in 1759 and grew up in the Bengal region of India.
He served in the Bengal army and came to Britain in 1782.
He then moved to Ireland and eloped with an Irish girl called Jane Daly in 1786, returning to England at
the turn of the century. In 1810 he opened the Hindoostane Coffee House in George Street, London.
It was the first curry house to open in Britain.
Mahomet and his wife also introduced 'shampooing', the Indian art of head massage, to Britain.

ISAMBARD KINGDOM BRUNEL
(1806-1859)
- Brunel was originally from Portsmouth, England. He was an engineer who built tunnels, bridges,
railway lines and ships. He was responsible for constructing the Great Western Railway,
which was the first major railway built in Britain. It runs from Paddington Station in London to the south
west of England, the West Midlands and Wales. Many of Brunel's bridges are still in use today.
He designed the Clifton Suspension Bridge, spanning the Avon Gorge.

FLORENCE NIGHTINGALE
(1820-1910)
- Florence Nightingale was born in Italy to English parents. At the age of thirty-one (31),
she was trained as a nurse in Germany. In 1854, she went to Turkey and worked in military hospitals,
treating soldiers who were fighting in the Crimean War. She and her fellow nurses improved the conditions
in the hospital and reduced the mortality rate. In 1860, she established the Nightingale Training School for
nurses at St Thomas' Hospital in London. The school was the first of its kind and still exists today,
as do many of the practices that Florence used. She is often regarded as the founder of modern nursing.

EMMELINE PANKHURST
(1858-1928)
- Emmeline Pankhurst was born in Manchester in 1858.
  She set up the Women's Franchise League in 1889,
  which fought to get the vote in local elections for married women.

- In 1903, she helped found the Women's Social and Political Union (WSPU).
  This was the first group whose members were called 'suffragettes'.
  The group used civil disobedience as part of their protest to gain the vote for women.
  They chained themselves to railings, smashed windows and committed arson.
  Many of the women, including Emmeline, went on hunger strike.

- In 1918, women over the age of thirty (30) were given voting rights and the right to stand for Parliament,
  partly in recognition of the contribution women made to the war effort during the First World War.
  Shortly before Emmeline's death in 1928, women were given the right to vote at the age of twenty-one (21),
  the same as men.

RUDYARD KIPLING
(1865-1936)
- Rudyard Kipling was born in India in 1865 and later lived in India, the UK and the USA.
  He wrote books and poems set in both India and the UK.

- His poems and novels reflected the idea that the British Empire was a force for good.
  Kipling was awarded the Nobel Prize in Literature in 1907.
  His books include the : Just So Stories and The Jungle Book, which continue to be popular today.

- His poem 'If' has often been voted among the UK's favourite poems.
  It begins with these words :
  'If you can keep your head when all about you
   Are losing theirs and blaming it on you ;
   If you can trust yourself when all men doubt you,
   But make allowance for their doubting too ;
   If you can wait and not be tired by waiting,
   Or being lied about, don't deal in lies,
   Or being hated, don't give way to hating,
   And yet don't look too good, nor talk too wise'

WINSTON CHURCHILL
(1874-1965)

- Churchill was the son of a politician and,
  before becoming a Conservative MP in 1900, was a soldier and journalist.

- In May 1940 he became Prime Minister.
  He refused to surrender to the Nazis and was an inspirational leader to the British people in a time of great hardship. He lost the General Election in 1945 but returned as Prime Minister in 1951.

- He was an MP until he stood down at the 1964 General Election.
  Following his death in 1965, he was given a state funeral.
  He remains a much-admired figure to this day, and in 2002 was voted the greatest Briton of all time by the public. Winston Churchill, best known for his leadership of the UK during the Second World War.

- During the War, he made many famous speeches including lines which you may still hear :

  'I have nothing to offer but blood, toil, tears and sweat'
  Churchill's first speech to the House of Commons after he became Prime Minister, 1940.

  'We shall fight on the beaches,
  we shall fight on the landing grounds,
  we shall fight in the fields and in the streets,
  we shall fight in the hills ;
  we shall never surrender'
  Speech to the House of Commons after Dunkirk, 1940.

  'Never in the field of human conflict was so much owed by so many to so few'
  Speech to the House of Commons during the Battle of Britain, 1940.

ALEXANDER FLEMING
(1881-1955)

- Born in Scotland, Fleming moved to London as a teenager and later qualified as a doctor.
  He was researching influenza (the 'flu') in 1928 when he discovered penicillin.
  This was then further developed into a usable drug by the scientists Howard Florey and Ernst Chain.
  By the 1940s it was in mass production. Fleming won the Nobel Prize in Medicine in 1945.
  Penicillin is still used to treat bacterial infections today.

CLEMENT ATTLEE
(1883-1967)
- Clement Attlee was born in London in 1883.
  His father was a solicitor and, after studying at Oxford University, Attlee became a barrister.
  He gave this up to do social work in East London and eventually became a Labour MP.
  He was Winston Churchill's Deputy Prime Minister in the wartime coalition government and
  became Prime Minister after the Labour Party won the 1945 election.

- He was Prime Minister from 1945 to 1951 and led the Labour Party for twenty (20) years.
  Attlee's government undertook the nationalisation of major industries (like coal and steel), created
  the National Health Service and implemented many of Beveridge's plans for a stronger welfare state.
  Attlee also introduced measures to improve the conditions of workers.

WILLIAM BEVERIDGE
(1879-1963)
- William Beveridge (later Lord Beveridge) was a British economist and social reformer.
  He served briefly as a Liberal MP and was subsequently the leader of the Liberals in the House of Lords
  but is best known for the 1942 report Social Insurance and Allied Services known as the **Beveridge Report**.

- The report was commissioned by the wartime government in 1941.
  It recommended that the government should find ways of fighting the five (5) 'Giant Evils' of :
  Want, Disease, Ignorance, Squalor and Idleness and provided the basis of the modern welfare state.

RICHARD AUSTEN BUTLER
(1902-1982)
- Richard Austen Butler (later Lord Butler) was born in 1902.
  He became a Conservative MP in 1923 and held several positions before becoming responsible for
  education in 1941. In this role, he oversaw the introduction of the Education Act 1944 often
  called 'The Butler Act', which introduced free secondary education in England and Wales.

- The education system has changed significantly since the Act was introduced, but the division
  between primary and secondary schools that it enforced still remains in most areas of Britain.

DYLAN THOMAS
(1914-1953)
- Dylan Thomas was a Welsh poet and writer. He often read and performed his work in public, including for the BBC. His most well-known works include the radio play Under Milk Wood, first performed after his death in 1954, and the poem Do Not Go Gentle Into That Good Night which he wrote for his dying father in 1952. He died at the age of thirty-nine (39) in New York. There are several memorials to him in his birthplace, Swansea, including a statue and the Dylan Thomas Centre.

MARY PETERS
(1939-)
- Born in Manchester, Mary Peters moved to Northern Ireland as a child. She was a talented athlete who won an Olympic gold medal in the pentathlon in 1972. After this, she raised money for local athletics and became the team manager for the women's British Olympic team. She continues to promote sport and tourism in Northern Ireland and was made a Dame of the British Empire in 2000 in recognition of her work.

MARGARET THATCHER
(1925-2013)
- Margaret Thatcher was the daughter of a grocer from Grantham in Lincolnshire.
  She trained as a chemist and lawyer. She was elected as a Conservative MP in 1959 and became a cabinet minister in 1970 as the Secretary of State for Education and Science. In 1975 she was elected as Leader of the Conservative Party and so became Leader of the Opposition. Following the Conservative victory in the General Election in 1979, Margaret Thatcher became the first woman Prime Minister of the UK.

- She was the longest-serving Prime Minister of the 20th century, remaining in office until 1990. During her premiership, there were a number of important economic reforms within the UK. She worked closely with the United States President, Ronald Reagan, and was one of the first Western leaders to recognise and welcome the changes in the leadership of the Soviet Union which eventually led to the end of the Cold War.

ROALD DAHL
(1916-1990)
- Roald Dahl was born in Wales to Norwegian parents. He served in the Royal Air Force during the Second World War. It was during the 1940s that he began to publish books and short stories.
  He is most well known for his children's books, although he also wrote for adults.
  His best-known works include : Charlie and the Chocolate Factory, and George's Marvellous Medicine.
  Several of his books have been made into films.

SOME GREAT BRITISH INVENTIONS OF THE 20TH CENTURY

JOHN LOGIE BAIRD

(1888-1946)

- TELEVISION
  The television was developed by Scotsman John Logie Baird in the 1920s.
  In 1932 he made the first television broadcast between London and Glasgow.

SIR ROBERT WATSON-WATT

(1892-1973)

- RADAR
  Radar was developed by Scotsman Sir Robert Watson-Watt who proposed that enemy aircraft
  could be detected by radio waves. The first successful radar test took place in 1935.

SIR BERNARD LOVELL

(1913-2012)

- RADIO TELESCOPE
  Working with radar led Sir Bernard Lovell to make new discoveries in astronomy.
  The radio telescope he built at Jodrell Bank in Cheshire was for many years the biggest in the world
  and continues to operate today.

ALAN TURING

(1912-1954)

- TURING MACHINE
  A Turing machine is a theoretical mathematical device invented by Alan Turing,
  a British mathematician, in the 1930s.
  The theory was influential in the development of computer science and the modern-day computer.

JOHN MACLEOD

(1876-1935)

- INSULIN
  The Scottish physician and researcher John Macleod was the co-discoverer of insulin,
  used to treat diabetes.

FRANCIS CRICK

(1916-2004)
- STRUCTURE OF THE DNA MOLECULE
  The structure of the DNA molecule was discovered in 1953 through work at British universities in London and Cambridge. This discovery contributed to many scientific advances, particularly in medicine and fighting crime. Francis Crick, one of those awarded the Nobel Prize for this discovery, was British.

SIR FRANK WHITTLE

(1907-1996)
- JET ENGINE
  The jet engine was developed in Britain in the 1930s by Sir Frank Whittle, a British Royal Air Force engineer officer.

SIR CHRISTOPHER COCKERELL

(1910-1999)
- HOVERCRAFT
  Sir Christopher Cockerell, is a British inventor, invented the hovercraft in the 1950s.

BRITAIN AND FRANCE

- CONCORDE AIRCRAFT
  British and France developed Concorde, the world's only supersonic passenger aircraft.
  It first flew in 1969 and began carrying passengers in 1976.
  Concorde was retired from service in 2003.

- HARRIER JUMP JET
  The Harrier jump jet, an aircraft capable of taking off vertically,
  was also designed and developed in the UK.

JAMES GOODFELLOW

(1937-)
- CASH DISPENSING ATM (AUTOMATIC TELLER MACHINE)
  In the 1960s, James Goodfellow invented the cash-dispensing ATM (automatic teller machine) or 'cashpoint'. The first of these was put into use by Barclays Bank in Enfield, north London in 1967.

SIR ROBERT EDWARDS
(1925-)
PATRICK STEPTOE
(1913-1988)
- IVF (IN-VITRO FERTILISATION) THERAPY
  IVF for the treatment of infertility was pioneered in Britain by physiologist Sir Robert Edwards and gynaecologist Patrick Steptoe. The world's first 'test-tube baby' was born in Oldham, Lancashire in 1978.

SIR IAN WILMOT
(1944-)
KEITH CAMPBELL
(1954-2012)
- CLONING
  In 1996, two (2) British scientists, Sir Ian Wilmot and Keith Campbell, led a team which was the first to succeed in cloning a mammal, Dolly the sheep. This has led to further research into the possible use of cloning to preserve endangered species and for medical purposes.

SIR PETER MANSFIELD
(1933-)
- MRI (MAGNETIC RESONANCE IMAGING) SCANNER
  A British scientist, is the co-inventor of the MRI (magnetic resonance imaging) scanner.
  This enables doctors and researchers to obtain exact and non-invasive images of human internal organs and has revolutionised diagnostic medicine.

SIR TIM BERNERS-LEE
(1955-)
- WORLD WIDE WEB
  The inventor of the world wide web (www), Sir Tim Berners-Lee is British.
  Information was successfully transferred via the web for the first time on 25 December 1990.

NOTABLE BRITISH SPORTSMEN AND WOMEN

SIR ROGER BANNISTER
(1929-)
* was the first man in the world to run a mile in under four (4) minutes, in 1954.

SIR JACKIE STEWART
(1939-)
* is a Scottish former racing driver who won the Formula 1 World Championship three (3) times.

BOBBY MOORE
(1941-1993)
* captained the English football team that won the World Cup in 1966.

SIR IAN BOTHAM
(1955-)
* captained the English cricket team and holds a number English Test cricket records, both for batting and for bowling.

JAYNE TORVILL
(1957-)
CHRISTOPHER DEAN
(1958-)
* won gold medals for ice dancing at the Olympic Games in 1984 and in four (4) consecutive world championships.

SIR STEVE REDGRAVE
(1962-)
* won gold medals in rowing in five (5) consecutive Olympic Games and is one of Britain's greatest Olympians.

BARONESS TANNI GREY-THOMPSON

(1969-)

- is an athlete who uses a wheelchair and won sixteen (16) Paralympic medals, including eleven (11) gold medals, in races over five (5) Paralympic Games. She won the London Marathon six (6) times and broke a total of thirty (30) world records.

DAME KELLY HOLMES

(1970-)

- won two (2) gold medals for running in the 2004 Olympic Games. She has held a number of British and European records.

DAME ELLEN MACARTHUR

(1976-)

- is a yachtswoman and in 2004 became the fastest person to sail around the world singlehanded.

SIR CHRIS HOY

(1976-)

- is a Scottish cyclist who has won six (6) gold and one (1) silver Olympic medals. He has also won eleven (11) world championship titles.

DAVID WEIR

(1979-)

- is a Paralympian who uses a wheelchair and has won six (6) gold medals over two (2) Paralympic Games. He has also won the London Marathon six (6) times.

SIR BRADLEY WIGGINS

(1980-)

- is a cyclist. In 2012, he became the first Briton to win the Tour de France. He has won seven (7) Olympic medals, including gold medals in the 2004, 2008 and 2012 Olympic Games.

MO FARAH

(1983-)
- is a British distance runner, born in Somalia.
  He won gold medals in the 2012 Olympics for the five thousand (5,000) and ten thousand (10,000) metres and is the first Briton to win the Olympic gold medal in the ten thousand (10,000) metres.

JESSICA ENNIS

(1986-)
- is an athlete. She won the 2012 Olympic gold medal in the heptathlon, which includes seven (7) different track and field events. She also holds a number of British athletics records.

ANDY MURRAY

(1987-)
- is a Scottish tennis player who in 2012 won the men's singles in the US Open.
  He is the first British man to win a singles title in a Grand Slam tournament since 1936.
  In the same year, he won Olympic gold and silver medals and was runner-up in the men's singles at Wimbledon.

ELLIE SIMMONDS

(1994-)
- is a Paralympian who won gold medals for swimming at the 2008 and 2012 Paralympic Games and holds a number of world records. She was the youngest member of the British team at the 2008 Games.

NOTABLE COMPOSERS

HENRY PURCELL
(1659-1695)
* was the organist at Westminster Abbey.
  He wrote church music, operas and other pieces, and developed a British style distinct from that elsewhere in Europe. He continues to be influential on British composers.

GEORGE FREDERICK HANDEL
(1685-1759)
* the German-born composer, spent many years in the UK and became a British citizen in 1727.
  He wrote the :
  Water Music for King George I and Music for the Royal Fireworks (for his son, George II).
  Both these pieces continue to be very popular.

* Handel also wrote an oratorio, Messiah, which is sung regularly by choirs, often at Easter time.

MORE RECENT, IMPORTANT COMPOSERS

GUSTAV HOLST
(1874-1934)
- More recently, important composers include Gustav Holst, whose work includes The Planets,
  a suite of pieces themed around the planets of the solar system. He adapted Jupiter,
  part of the Planets suite, as the tune for I Vow to Thee My Country, a popular hymn in British churches.

SIR EDWARD ELGAR
(1857-1934)
- was born in Worcester, England.
  His best-known work is probably the Pomp and Circumstance Marches. March No 1
  (Land of Hope and Glory) is usually played at the Last Night of the Proms at the Royal Albert Hall.

RALPH VAUGHAN WILLIAMS
(1872-1958)
- wrote music for orchestras and choirs. He was strongly influenced by traditional English folk music.

SIR WILLIAM WALTON
(1902-1983)
- wrote a wide range of music, from film scores to opera. He wrote marches for the coronations of
  King George VI and Queen Elizabeth the II but his best-known works are probably :
  Facade, which became a ballet, and Balthazar's Feast, which is intended to be sung by a large choir.

BENJAMIN BRITTEN
(1913-1976)
- is best known for his operas, which include Peter Grimes and Billy Budd.
  He also wrote A Young Person's Guide to the Orchestra, which is based on a piece of music by Purcell
  and introduces the listener to the various different sections of an orchestra.
  He founded the Aldeburgh Festival in Suffolk, which continues to be a popular music event of international
  importance.

NOTABLE BRITISH ARTISTS

THOMAS GAINSBOROUGH
(1727-1788)
- was a portrait painter who often painted people in the country or garden scenery.

DAVID ALLAN
(1744-1796)
- was a Scottish painter who was best known for painting portraits.
  One of his most famous works is called The Origin of Painting.

JOSEPH TURNER
(1775-1851)
- was an influential landscape painter in a modern style.
  He is considered the artist who raised the profile of landscape painting.

JOHN CONSTABLE
(1776-1837)
- was a landscape painter most famous for his works of Dedham Vale on the Suffolk-Essex border
  in the east of England.

THE PRE-RAPHAELITES
- were an important group of artists in the second half of the 19th century.
  They painted detailed pictures on religious or literary themes in bright colours.
  The group included : Holman Hunt, Dante Gabriel Rossetti and Sir John Millais.

SIR JOHN LAVERY
(1856-1941)
- was a very successful Northern Irish portrait painter. His work included painting the Royal Family.

HENRY MOORE
(1898-1986)
- was an English sculptor and artist. He is best known for his large bronze abstract sculptures.

JOHN PETTS
(1914-1991)
- was a Welsh artist, best known for his engravings and stained glass.

LUCIAN FREUD
(1922-2011)
- was a German-born British artist. He is best known for his portraits.

DAVID HOCKNEY
(1937-)
- was an important contributor to the 'pop art' movement of the 1960s and continues to be influential today.

NOTABLE AUTHORS AND WRITERS

JANE AUSTEN
(1775-1817)
- was an English novelist. Her books include : Pride and Prejudice, and Sense and Sensibility.
  Her novels are concerned with marriage and family relationships.
  Many have been made into television programmes or films.

CHARLES DICKENS
(1812-1870)
- wrote a number of very famous novels, including : Oliver Twist, and Great Expectations.
  You will hear references in everyday talk to some of the characters in his books, such as :
  Scrooge (a mean person) or Mr Micawber (always hopeful).

ROBERT LOUIS STEVENSON
(1850-1894)
- wrote books which are still read by adults and children today.
  His most famous books include : Treasure Island, Kidnapped, and Dr Jekyll and Mr Hyde.

THOMAS HARDY
(1840-1928)
- was an author and poet. His best-known novels focus on rural society and include :
  Far from the Madding Crowd, and Jude the Obscure.

SIR ARTHUR CONAN DOYLE
(1859-1930)
- was a Scottish doctor and writer. He was best known for his stories about Sherlock Holmes,
  who was one of the first fictional detectives.

EVELYN WAUGH
(1903-1966)
- wrote satirical novels, including Decline and Fall, and Scoop.
  He is perhaps best known for Brideshead Revisited.

SIR KINGSLEY AMIS
(1922-1995)
- was an English novelist and poet. He wrote more than twenty (20) novels.
  The most well known is Lucky Jim.

GRAHAM GREENE
(1904-1991)
- wrote novels often influenced by his religious beliefs, including :
  The Heart of the Matter, The Honorary Consul, Brighton Rock, and Our Man in Havana.

J K ROWLING
(1965-)
- wrote the Harry Potter series of children's books, which have enjoyed huge international success.
  She now writes fiction for adults as well.

SOME FAMOUS LINES

ROBERT BROWNING
(1812-1889)

HOME THOUGHTS FROM ABROAD
'Oh, to be in England now that April's there
And whoever wakes in England sees, some morning, unaware,
That the lowest boughs and the brushwood sheaf
Round the elm-tree bole are in tiny leaf
While the Chaffinch sings on the orchard bough
In England - Now!'

LORD BYRON
(1788-1824)

SHE WALKS IN BEAUTY
'She walks in beauty, like the night
Of cloudless climes and starry skies ;
And all that's best of dark and bright
Meet in her aspect and her eyes'

WILLIAM WORDSWORTH
(1770-1850)

THE DAFFODILS
'I wander'd lonely as a cloud
That floats on high o'er vales and hills,
When all at once I saw a crowd,
A host of golden daffodils'

WILLIAM BLAKE
(1757-1827)

THE TYGER
'Tyger! Tyger! Burning bright
 In the forests of the night,
 What immortal hand or eye
 Could frame thy fearful symmetry?'

WILFRED OWEN
(1893-1918)

ANTHEM FOR DOOMED YOUTH
'What passing-bells for these who die as cattle?
 Only the monstrous anger of the guns.
 Only the stuttering rifles' rapid rattle
 Can patter out their hasty orisons.'

SOME FAMOUS BRITISH FILMS

The 39 Steps	1935	directed by **Alfred Hitchcock**
Brief Encounter	1945	directed by **David Lean**
The Third Man	1949	directed by **Carol Reed**
The Belles of St Trinian's	1954	directed by **Frank Launder**
Lawrence of Arabia	1962	directed by **David Lean**
Women in Love	1969	directed by **Ken Russell**
Don't Look Now	1973	directed by **Nicolas Roeg**
Chariots of Fire,	1981	directed by **Hugh Hudson**
The Killing Fields	1984	directed by **Roland Joffe**
Four Weddings and a Funeral	1994	directed by **Mike Newell**
Touching the Void	2003	directed by **Kevin MacDonald**

ANNEX

GLOSSARY
ABOUT THE AUTHOR
ACKNOWLEDGEMENT

GLOSSARY

When words may be difficult to understand, an example of use may follow the definition.
The word that is bracketed after an entry relates to the particular context in which the word is being defined - for example : arrested (police). A slash (/) separates different definition.

AD
Anno Domini - referring to the number of years after the birth of Jesus Christ - used as a time reference.

allegiance
Loyalty to something - for example : to a leader, a faith, or a country.

armed forces
The army, navy and air force which defend a country in times of peace and war.

arrested (police)
Taken by the police to a police station and made to stay there to answer questions about illegal actions or activity.

assault
The criminal act of using physical force against someone or of attacking someone - for example : hitting someone.

bank holiday
A day when most people have an official day off work and many businesses are closed.
A bank holiday can also be called a public holiday.

baron
A man who has one of the ranks of the British nobility.
The title was particularly common during the Middle Ages.

BC
Before Christ - referring to the number of years before Jesus Christ was born - used as a time reference.

bishop
A senior member of the clergy in the Christian religion, often in charge of the churches in a particular area.

boom
A sharp rise in something - very often in business activity or the economy.

brutality
Behaviour towards another which is cruel and violent and causes harm.

by-election
An election held in a parliamentary constituency or local authority area to fill a vacancy.

cabinet (government)
A group of senior ministers who are responsible for controlling government policy.

casualties (medical)
People who are wounded or killed - for example : in a war.

charter (government)
An official written statement which describes the rights and responsibilities of a state and its citizens.

chieftain
The leader of a clan in Scotland or Ireland.

civil disobedience
The refusal of members of the public to obey laws, often because they want to protest against political issues.

civil law
The legal system that deals with disputes between people or groups of people.

civil service
The departments within the government which manage the business of running the country - people who work for the government can be called civil servants.

civil war
A war between groups who live in the same country.

clan
A group of people or families who live under the rule of a chieftain and may be descendants of the same person - a term used traditionally in Scotland.

clergy
Religious leaders, used here to describe religious leaders in Christian churches.

coalition
A partnership between different political parties.

colonise
Inhabit and take control of another country. People who colonise are called colonists.

commemorate
Show that something or someone is remembered.

conquered
Beaten in battle.

constituency
A specific area where the voters who live in that place (its constituents) can elect an MP to represent them in Parliament.

constitution (law)
The legal structure of established laws and principles which is used to govern a country.

convention (government)
An agreement, often between countries, about particular rules or codes of behaviour.

criminal law
The legal system that deals with illegal activities.

decree (law)
Official order, law or decision.

democratic country
A country which is governed by people who are elected by the population to represent them in Parliament.

devolution
The passing of power from a central government to another group at a regional or local level, which can then be called a devolved administration.

dialect
A form of a language spoken by a particular group or people living in a particular area.

domestic policies
Political decisions that relate to what is happening within a country (as opposed to in another country).

electoral register
The official list of all the people in a country who are allowed to vote in an election.

electorate
All the people who are allowed to vote in an election.

eligible
Allowed by law.

ethnic origin
The country of birth, someone's race or the nationality of someone when they were born /
the customs and place from which a person and their family originated (or came from).

executed
Killed as a punishment.

first past the post
A system of election in which the candidate with the largest number of votes in a particular constituency
wins a seat in Parliament.

franchise
The right to vote.

General Election
An event in which all the citizens of a country who are allowed to vote,
choose the people they wish to represent them in their government.

government policies
Official ideas and beliefs that are agreed by a political party about how to govern the country.

guilty
Found by a court to have done something which is illegal.

heir
Someone who will legally receive a person's money or possessions after their death.
The heir to the throne is the person who will become the next king or queen.

House (history)
A family - for example : House of York.

House of Commons
That part of the Houses of Parliament where MPs who are elected by the voting public debate political issues.

House of Lords
That part of the Houses of Parliament where people who have inherited their place or been chosen by the government debate political issues.

household
A home and the people who live in it / something that relates to a home -
for example : household chores are tasks that are done around the house, such as cleaning and cooking.

Houses of Parliament
The building in London where the House of Commons and the House of Lords meet.

illegal
Something which the law does not allow.

infrastructure
Structured network that is necessary for successful operation of a business or transport system -
for example : roads or railways.

innocent (law)
Found by a court not to have done something illegal.

judge
The most important official in court.
The judge makes sure what happens in court is fair and legal.

judiciary
All the judges in a country.
Together, they are responsible for using the law of the land in the correct way.

jury (legal)
People who are chosen to sit in court, listen to information about a crime,
and decide if someone is guilty or innocent.

legal
Allowed to do so by law.

legislative power
The power to make laws.

liberty
Freedom.

magistrate
A person who acts as a judge in a court case where the crime is not a serious one.

marital status
Information about whether a person is single, married, separated or divorced.
This is often asked for on official forms.

media, the
All the organisations which give information to the public,
i.e. newspapers, magazines, television, radio and the internet.

Medieval / Middle Ages
In history, the period between 1066 and about 1500.

monarch
The king or queen of a country.

national issues
Political problems that can affect everyone who lives in a country.

nationalised
Bought and then controlled by central government -
relating to an industry or service that was previously owned privately.

nobility
The people in a country who belong to the highest social class, some of whom may have titles - for example : Lord, Duke, Baron.

office, to be in
To be in power in government.

Olympics
International sporting event held every four (4) years.

opposition
In the House of Commons, the largest political party which is not part of the government is officially known as the opposition.

Pale (history)
Part of Ireland governed by the English.

party politics
The shared ideas and beliefs of an organised group of politicians.

patron saint
A Christian saint who is believed to protect a particular area or group of people.

penalty (law)
Punishment for breaking the law.

Pope, the
The head of the Roman Catholic Church.

practise a religion
Live according to the rules and beliefs of a religion.

Prime Minister
The politician who leads the government.

prohibit / prohibition
Make something illegal.

proportional representation
A system of election in which political parties are allowed a number of seats in Parliament that represents their share of the total number of votes cast.

Protestants
Christians who are not members of the Roman Catholic Church.

public body
A governmental department or a group of people who represent or work for the government and who work for the good of the general public.

public house / pub
A place where adults can buy and drink alcohol.

Reformation, the
The religious movement in the 16th century that challenged the authority of the Pope and established Protestant churches in Europe.

refugee
A person who must leave the country where they live, often because of a war or for political reasons.

residence
The place where someone lives.

rival viewpoints
Opinions held by different groups of people.

rural
Countryside.

scrutinise
Examine all the details.

seat (Parliament)
A constituency.

sentence
A punishment imposed by a court.

shadow cabinet
Senior MPs of a political party not in government.

sheriff (law)
A judge in Scotland.

slavery
A system in which people bought and sold other people (slaves) who were forced to work without pay.

sonnet
A poem which is fourteen (14) lines long and rhymes in a particular way.

Speaker, the
The member of the House of Commons who controls the way issues are debated in Parliament.

stand for office
Apply to be elected - for example : as an MP or councillor.

strike, to go on
Refuse to work in order to protest against something.

successor (government)
A person who comes after another and takes over an office or receives some kind of power - for example : a son who becomes king when his father dies is his successor.

suspend
To stop something from happening or operating, usually for a short time.

terrorism
Violence used by people who want to force a government to do something.
The violence is usually random and unexpected, so that no one can feel really safe from it.

The Phone Book
A book which contains names, addresses and phone numbers of organisations, businesses and individuals.

theft
The criminal act of stealing something from a person, building or place.

trade union
An association of workers formed to protect its members.

treaty
An official written agreement between countries or governments.

uprising
A violent revolt or rebellion against an authority.

voluntary work
Work which someone does because they want to and which they do for free,
i.e. they do not receive any payment.

volunteer
Someone who works for free or who offers to do something without payment.

war effort
The work people did in order to help the country in any way they could during wartime.

Yellow Pages
A book that lists names, addresses and telephone numbers of businesses,
services and organisations in an area.
Also available online at : www.yell.com

ABOUT THE AUTHOR

Blesilda Zarate-Robb was initially granted Indefinite Leave to Remain and is now a naturalised British citizen. She is an architect originally from the Philippines, who has also self-published a pocket-sized book History of Architecture 'myboardbook' for the Architect Licensure Examination takers in the Philippines.

The life she led there was not that different but it was quite a challenge for her to start a new life in the UK. It is not what she is used to. The environment is all new and the weather is challenging!

Independent and adventurous as she is, she learnt to adjust quickly. Her values, positive outlook and willing heart were contributory to finding her feet in the UK. She is a very determined individual who blends in in no time. Her penchant to experiment, learn new things and come up with something is her trademark. She believes in 'give and take' and this 'Life in the UK Test Made Easy 3rd Edition' handbook reflects her desire to help and to give something back.

ACKNOWLEDGEMENT

A special thank you to Mr Gregory Robb, my husband, who has encouraged and inspired me to press on and do another version. If not for him I would not have done this book and I would not be here in the first place. He is both my critic and mentor - particularly on the technical aspect, which has made this book possible.

A big 'thank you' to the UK government for its migration policies, enabling me to become part of UK society, and to The Stationery Office (TSO) formerly Her Majesty's Stationery Office (HMSO) for the available material through the Open Government Licence.

Thank you also with all my heart to my parents,
Mr Benjamin and Mrs Flordeliza Zarate - instrumental in who and what I have become.